Customer Oriented Software Quality Assurance

Frank P. Ginac

To join a Prentice Hall PTR internet mailing list, point to
http://www.prenhall.com/mail_lists/

ISBN 0-13-571464-8

Prentice Hall PTR
Upper Saddle River
New Jersey 07458

Library of Congress Cataloging in Publication Data

Ginac, Frank
    Customer-oriented software quality assurance / Frank P. Ginac.
        p.   cm
    Includes index.
    ISBN 0-13-571464-8
    1. computer software--Quality control. 2. Quality assurance. I. Title.
QA76.76.Q35G49   1997
005.3--dc21   97-45523
                                        CIP

Editorial/Production Supervision: *Joanne Anzalone*
Acquisitions Editor: *Bernard Goodwin*
Cover Design Director: *Jerry Votta*
Cover Design: *Scott Weiss*
Manufacturing Manager: *Alexis R. Heydt*
Marketing Manager: *Miles Williams*
Editorial Assistant: *Diane Spina*

© 1998 Prentice Hall PTR
Prentice-Hall, Inc.
Upper Saddle River, New Jersey 07458

Prentice Hall books are widely used by corporations and government agencies for training, marketing, and resale.

The publisher offers discounts on this book when ordered in bulk quantities. For more information, contact: Corporate Sales Department, Phone: 800-382-3419; FAX: 201-236-7141; E-mail: corpsales@prenhall.com
Or write: Corp. Sales Dept., Prentice Hall PTR,
1 Lake Street, Upper Saddle River, NJ 07458

Printed in the United States of America
10 9 8 7 6 5

ISBN 0-13-571464-8

Reprinted with corrections September, 2000.

Prentice-Hall International (UK) Limited, *London*
Prentice-Hall of Australia Pty. Limited, *Sydney*
Prentice-Hall Canada Inc., *Toronto*
Prentice-Hall Hispanoamericana, S.A., *Mexico*
Prentice-Hall of India Private Limited, *New Delhi*
Prentice-Hall of Japan, Inc., *Tokyo*
Prentice-Hall Asia Pte. Ltd., *Singapore*
Editora Prentice-Hall do Brasil, Ltda., *Rio de Janeiro*

To my wife Linda
—the passion behind our success

Contents

Chapter 2
Building the Quality Attributes Set,   21

Chapter 3
Quality Metrics,   47

Chapter 4
Test Methods, Types, and Tools,   77

Chapter 5

The QA Program, 95

Chapter 6

Appraisal Programs, 119

In the Eyes of the Beholder

"The customer is the ultimate judge of product quality"

Ask a software developer to justify a claim that their company produces quality products. They will likely tell you, "We follow coding standards and hold code inspections, our organization is registered to ISO 9000, we eliminate all known defects before shipping a product, and each product is thoroughly tested. Our tests cover 95 percent of the code!" Quality is defined in terms of the processes used to develop and test their products, the test methodologies followed, test procedures employed, and empirical test data. Statements such as, "We pushed the system to its limits for 24 hours and encountered no failures," "we ran the regression test suite and discovered no defects," and "we went through four beta test cycles that lasted over two years," are often made to support the claim. Now ask that same software developer to think of a quality software product, or any quality product for that matter, that they've recently purchased. Then ask them to define quality as it applies to that product. Most likely, their reply will include statements that have little or nothing to do with processes, procedures, and test results. As a customer, they are more concerned with such things as the product's reliability, availability, performance, and the responsiveness of the company's service and support organizations. Statements such as, "All of the defects have been eliminated" and "it was thoroughly tested" are replaced by, "It is one of the easiest products that I have ever used," "I really like the way they've organized the toolbars," or, "I called their help hotline and received a quick answer to my installation question!"

Customers tend to define quality in terms of attributes that the product and the company producing the product possess, such as, it's easy to use, it's well packaged, or service and support are impressive. Another way to look at this is to think of each attribute as one element of a set that represents their definition of quality. Unfortunately, these quality attributes are often completely ignored by the company developing the product. Instead, the company's quality assurance (QA) goals and objectives are set based on an internal definition of quality that is often mandated in a corporate standards document that dictates criteria, such as, 85 percent code coverage and no severity one defects (a severity one defect is often defined to be a defect where a product feature or function is nonoperable).

If you accept the premise that your customers are the ultimate judge of your product's quality and you don't know their definition of quality, then how can you ever hope to produce a quality product? In this book, you will learn how to build a QA program that is based first on *their* definition of quality. I refer to this methodology as "customer-oriented software quality assurance."

This book addresses and provides a means by which an organization can solve several common problems faced when producing software products:

- Complex software systems having hundreds of millions of possible test cases and test scenarios are rarely if ever completely tested due to the practical constraints of time and resources. How does one select a sufficient subset of tests and test scenarios so that the quality of the end product satisfies the customer?

- Metrics are used throughout the software industry to gauge product quality. A metric is a measurement with an associated desirable value. For example, the defects per thousand lines of code measurement has an associated desirable value of less than one defect per million lines of code. If a product has one defect per ten thousand lines of code, is its quality poor? Also, does this measurement ultimately mean anything? Or, is it more important to measure the impact those defects have on the customer as they use the product? How does one select the right metrics to gauge product quality?

- Tests are the primary means by which product quality is assessed. What does it mean when a test fails? Is the quality of the product poor? Perhaps, but ultimately, the value of a test lies in its ability to determine whether or not the product satisfies customer quality requirements. For example, is a test that places a load on the system five times greater than any customer will ever place on the system a good determinant of quality? How does one select the right tests to use?

• There are a number of popular quality assurance appraisal programs advocated today. Charged with selecting one, which is the best to follow?

The chapters of this book are presented in chronological order. Chapter 1 presents an example of a quality attributes set. The quality attributes set is the single most important element of the customer-oriented software quality assurance methodology. It embodies customer quality requirements for a particular product or family of related products. The book begins with an example of such a set that is used throughout the book to clarify the methodology. Chapter 2 defines the process of building the quality attributes set through the construction of the example set presented in the preceding chapter. Chapter 3 is all about quality metrics. The two goals for this chapter are to develop an understanding of and appreciation for metrics and other methods of analysis and to define a process that can be followed to build a set of specific metrics from a quality attributes set. Chapter 4 discusses test methods. The two goals of this chapter are to review various test methods and test types and to learn how to select the ones needed to develop a test suite that will determine whether or not the product being tested satisfies or exceeds customer quality requirements. Chapter 5 brings it all together by defining the QA program. The goal of this chapter is to examine various activities that can be engaged in and tools that can be used to assist with the production of a product that satisfies customer quality requirements. Finally,

Chapter 6 reviews two important process appraisal programs: one from the Software Engineering Institute (SEI) and the other from the International Organization for Standardization (ISO).

The primary audience for this book is anyone faced with the task of building products that must meet or exceed their customers' quality requirements. In terms of job titles, functions, and responsibilities, those who I suspect will benefit the most from reading this book include quality assurance managers, software test managers, software development managers, and their respective teams, and perhaps senior staff members such as directors or vice-presidents responsible for such functions.

Throughout my career, I have studied and applied a long list of methodologies, techniques, processes, and procedures, attempting to produce software products of the highest quality. Along the way, I began to ask myself: Which one is best? I wanted to settle on a particular one that I could apply over and over again to achieve consistently desirable results. As I gave this particular problem serious thought, it occurred to me that to achieve that goal I would first have to define "desirable results." Isn't the primary desired result to produce a product of the highest quality? Yes! But, what does that mean? I realized that I would have to find the elusive definition of quality before I could solve this mystery. This book is the end result of that effort. It's not based on extensive research conducted in libraries and research labs. It's based on years of ad-hoc research, trial and error, and my personal experiences.

It is time now to venture forth to design a customer-oriented software quality assurance program, one that will enable you to produce products that satisfy customer quality requirements. As you read, keep in mind that the effort put into producing such products is only one piece of a larger effort that brings a product from marketing to design to production to sales to distribution to the customer and then to support and finally back to marketing. These functions can be thought of as nodes connected along a circle. The success of a product and ultimately the company producing it is directly linked to the quality of the nodes that form this circle and the quality of the communications channels that bind them. If you neglect any one node or the associated communications channels, you run the risk of collapsing the circle, ostracizing your customers, and losing the game.

Chapter 1

Quality Attributes

"Quality as defined by your customers"

1.1   INTRODUCTION

My first job as a professional software engineer was with Data General Corporation (DG) in Westboro, Massachusetts. I was hired as a software quality assurance engineer in the AOS/VS Software Quality Assurance Group (AOS/VS was Data General's proprietary operating system). It was back in the days of the MV/10000, just a few years after the *Soul of a New Machine* was written by Tracy Kidder, which chronicled the development of DG's first 32 bit minicomputer known as the Eclipse. It was also shortly after IEEE's release of the

1

"Standard for Software Quality Assurance and Test Plans." In those days, I often found myself challenged by my developer counterparts to define quality. My peers and I held countless discussions arguing over various possible definitions, searching for a common definition that would satisfy everyone. In the end, though, we were unsuccessful.

My experience at Data General is not unique. Many in the industry were searching for that elusive definition. After years of trying and repeated failures an interesting trend developed. Companies began to ask their customers to define quality. They discovered that each had a different definition. Eventually, software developers and software quality assurance engineers began to accept the possibility that a common definition does not exist. And, that instead of trying to find one, they should ask their customers to define the term so that they could focus their efforts on building products that satisfy the best definiton rather than their own self-serving one.

How do your customers define quality? To answer that question, stop and think for a moment about products you have purchased for yourself that you consider to be quality products. Are they quality products because they require infrequent servicing? Are they easy to use? Are they easy to install? The answers to such questions form a set of "quality attributes" that describe one aspect of your product purchase requirements. To increase the likelihood that someone will

---

[1] Similar attributes sets that describe other aspects of your product purchase requirements exist, however, since the focus of this book is on quality, I've limited our discussion to the quality attributes set.

purchase a product of yours, that product must satisfy their quality requirements, that is, it must possess many, if not all, of the quality attributes found in their quality attributes set. I should note here that there are situations where someone will purchase a product that does not satisfy their quality requirements. For example, they may have an urgent need for a product and have little time to evaluate products from all vendors (if indeed there is more than one vendor!). If they happen to purchase a product from you that is of poor quality, they will certainly refrain from purchasing any other products from you once their crisis has passed. As an example, imagine living in Austin, Texas, on a balmy 110° day in the middle of August when suddenly your air conditioner is irreparably damaged by fire ants. The urgency of the situation has you running out to the nearest appliance store to buy a new air conditioner. Faced with many choices, you choose to purchase an affordable unit from a well-known company. You bring the unit home, install it, turn it on, and begin to cool down. The next day, after 24 hours of operation, the unit stops blowing cold air! In a panic, you call the repair person. After several minutes of examination you are informed that you have a defective compressor and that it will take a few days to get a new one. Would you ever buy a product from that company again?

The quality attributes set is a way to represent customer quality requirements. To create the quality attributes set, you must ask both your current and prospective customers to answer a number of questions that collectively ask the question, "How do you define quality?" By consolidating their responses, you will develop the set of quality attributes that describe their quality requirements. The process of building the quality attributes set is covered in depth in Chapter 2.

The remainder of this chapter presents an example of a quality attributes set and examines each element in detail. The example set presented in this chapter and used throughout the book is not based on a formal application of customer-oriented software quality assurance. In fact, there are no case studies to date! The individual elements of the set, however, are drawn from real experiences. The purpose of including an example is to put substance behind the description of the process, hopefully making it easier to understand and remember. Also, to further the cause of making the process described in this book comprehensible and easy to remember, it is described from the perspective of a fictitious company named COSQA Software (COSQA is short for Customer-Oriented Software Quality Assurance) that has applied it to one of their product development efforts.

The quality attributes presented in this example are unique to the customers polled for our fictitious company. You must determine for yourself the unique quality requirements of *your* customers. A customer-oriented software quality assurance program is designed to satisfy customer quality requirements as expressed by the quality attributes set.

1.2 THE QUALITY ATTRIBUTES SET

1.2.1 Product-Specific Attributes

1.2.1.1   Ease of Use

Have you ever used a product that seemed to have more controls than necessary, or controls placed in odd or awkward positions, or perhaps seemed to be missing controls? Have product-use procedures ever baffled you or made you feel like an idiot? Products like the VCR have long had terrible ease of use reputations. Have you ever tried to program your VCR to tape a show at a certain time, day, and channel while you're away? If your VCR has on-screen programming, perhaps, the procedure is tolerable. But, if you have an older VCR, like mine, then you find the task of programming it so counterintuitive and painful that you avoid this feature altogether.

Because ease of use is often such an important quality attribute, many manufacturers mention it in their advertisements and product information sheets as if it were a product feature. If you had to choose between two products that are identical in every way except that one is reported to be easy to use and the other as difficult, which one would you choose? Well, for some of you, the challenge of a difficult-to-use product may drive your decision to purchase the latter; however most would agree that the former would appeal to more customers.

COSQA Software's customers prefer to purchase software products that don't require them to read the manual or use the on-line help facilities. They look for products with Graphical User Interfaces (GUIs) that "look and feel" like other products that they use regularly, such as their word processors and spreadsheet programs. Those programs have what they call "intuitive" user interfaces, which is another way of saying that they can learn the product by playing with it for a short period of time without consulting the manual. They also prefer products that have a GUI that is sparsely populated with buttons and pop-up (or pulldown) menus, leaving a large work area in which they can create their frequent masterpieces.

1.2.1.2   Documentation

Incomplete, missing, inaccurate, and poorly translated documentation may lead many customers to conclude that a product is of poor quality. Documentation is usually an afterthought in product development efforts. Consequently, minimal time is spent developing it and ensuring that it is accurate. For some customers, this may not pose a problem. They rarely refer to the documentation, preferring to learn to use a product by trial and error. For others, however, the documentation is a vital part of their daily use of the product. Inaccuracies, missing information, and the like lead such a customer to experience unnecessary frustration that may drive them away from future purchases.

COSQA Software's customers expect all documentation to be on-line and context sensitive. They also prefer comprehensive and voluminous documentation. During the interviews, they noted that a quick-start or getting-started manual is indispensable. They cannot stand searching through documentation to figure out something as simple as installing the product, invoking it, and using its most elementary features. Also, they find errors in documentation inexcusable. They believe that any product with poorly edited documentation must contain coding errors that will someday surface at a most inopportune moment, destroying one of their works in progress. Fearing such a disaster, they may not purchase a product known to have poorly edited documentation.

1.2.1.3 Defect Tolerance

Put simply, a defect is an undesirable behavior or characteristic of a product. Some defects are more severe than others. For example, you are driving your car down the street and decide to adjust your side-view mirror—you have one of those mechanical mirror adjusters. Suddenly, you hear a snap and the control falls limp in your hand. Time for a new car? Probably not. If you are at all like me, you'll view it as an engineering challenge, a problem to be solved, and run home to open up that old tool box and put your skills as a backyard mechanic to the test. That sort of breakdown, though annoying, is not as severe as say, your engine suddenly seizing.

That reminds me of the time I owned a 1970 Volkswagen Beetle. It was the early eighties and I was driving my car home from college one weekend to get away from the madness known as Dickinson Hall at the University of Massachusetts in Amherst, MA. I stopped at a convenience store along the way for a cup of coffee— the trip home was long and boring enough to lull me into a catatonic state. When I returned to my car, I turned the key, the engine cranked over and over, but it wouldn't start. Now I don't know how many of you have had the pleasure of owning such a fine automobile, but let me tell you, it was the most reliable car I've ever owned. The floor was rotted out, it had no heater or defroster, and the muffler was shot, but it always started and carried me to my final destination.

This time, though, it wouldn't start. Something must be really wrong—a severe defect. Catastrophe had finally found me! Well, fortunately I kept my head and looked at the situation as another opportunity to flex my mechanical prowess. I opened up the rear engine cover, poked around for a few minutes, and discovered that the ignition wire had burned in half! I did what any other VW owner would have done in that situation. I took one of the spark plug wires and used it as the ignition wire. I drove home on three cylinders!

A broken mirror and a dead engine are two extremes of defect types. They illustrate an important point though: defects are never good, but some are less tolerable than others. You have to determine which types of defects fall under the class of tolerable and which ones fall under the class of intolerable. Your QA efforts should initially emphasize and focus on elimination and prevention of defects in the intolerable class.

To COSQA Software's customers, defects such as a few typos in message strings and in help text as well as minor disparities between documented and actual behavior or function will be tolerated until the next release. On the other hand, they will not tolerate defects that alter or destroy their works in progress or that adversely affect their productivity. Such defects will likely drive them to abandon the product in favor of a product that may be less robust but more reliable. They consider defects such as general exceptions, hangs, data corruption, and long delays between operations to be intolerable defects.

1.2.1.4   Defect Frequency

If you determine that a particular defect type is tolerable (you've interviewed your customers and they have told you that they would tolerate defects of that type,) but your customers encounter such a defect in your product with great frequency, it will likely become intolerable. If a defect becomes intolerable because of a high frequency of incidence, then elimination of these defects should become a priority.

Though COSQA Software's customers will tolerate a few misspelled words in a product's message strings and help text, they are unwilling to tolerate large numbers of misspelled words or typos. Minor defects that appear frequently end up distracting or frustrating them to the point that their productivity suffers and they consider anything that adversely affects their productivity to be an intolerable major defect.

1.2.1.5   Defect Impact

If a defect results in a brief operational delay, its effect may be negligible, that is, it may be tolerable to the customer. If, however, it results in long operational delays, it will most likely become intolerable. As an example, consider a large telemarketing company that relies upon a Database Management System (DBMS) application to record orders, make inquiries about the availability of a particular product, and check the status of an order. Their entire operation is built around this particular application. When it is down, their business

grinds to an abrupt halt. Let's say that each minute the
database is down represents $1,000,000 of lost revenue.
Consider next that while testing the system you discover a defect that at first glance appears to be of a tolerable nature. You discover that whenever another
application running on the system performs an I/O
(Input/Output) operation, the DBMS pauses briefly and
then resumes. Should you consider that brief pause an
intolerable defect? By itself, that brief pause may be
tolerable, but, if the other application were suddenly to
perform a long series of I/O operations that increased
the DBMS's pause to one minute, the defect would suddenly become intolerable.

COSQA Software's customers see themselves as
highly productive people who prefer to work on several
things at once. They often start several applications on
their workstations simultaneously, jumping from one to
another. Many of COSQA Software's customers have
had an experience where they noticed that whenever
they jumped from their word processor to a particular
vendor's desktop publishing system they have had to
wait several minutes for the view to redraw. The desktop publishing system developers decided to optimize
memory usage, thereby sacrificing view redrawing performance. They assumed that most users would not
switch from application to application while using their
product; consequently view redrawing would be infrequent. To save memory, they decided to save the current view on disk, retrieving it whenever they needed
to perform a redraw. This design decision saved a large
amount of memory but sacrificed redrawing performance. Though some users might appreciate the
designers' effort to decrease memory usage, COSQA

Software's customers viewed the resulting poor performance of view redrawing as a major defect since it severely impacted their productivity.

1.2.1.6 Packaging

Many customers believe that quality products are found only inside attractive packages. If the package is poorly designed, dull and uninteresting, shoddy, or made from inferior materials, they may reason that the product is also of poor quality. The product may or may not be of poor quality, but because of their beliefs, experiences, and prejudices, many customers initially judge the quality of the product based on its packaging.

The customers who were interviewed for COSQA Software's new product believe that quality software products are found only in large packages having substantial weight, that are covered with colorful award winning graphic designs and descriptions of the product's features in excruciating detail, and that are emblazoned with endorsements from the leading trade magazines. The box must be filled to capacity with floppies or CD-ROMs, lots of documentation, and offers for free demo software.

1.2.1.7 Price versus Reliability

How could a product's price possibly affect quality? It is not the cost of the product; rather, it is the expectation of quality as a function of the price the customer paid. High-priced items tend to set different expectations about quality than low-priced items. Be careful here, though. What is high priced to one person may not be to another. If you are selling products to a multibillion dollar enterprise, they may consider anything above $1,000,000 to be a high-priced item. On the other hand, a thousand dollar product may be considered high priced to a new one-person business with limited capital.

When a product is viewed as high priced by the customer, how are defects of a certain type viewed by them? To answer this question you have to place yourself in their shoes. Don't make the mistake of answering this question as if you were personally going to purchase this product using your own checking account. If the customer pays a premium for your product, their expectations about quality will affect their tolerance of defects of a certain type. The converse is also true. What is perceived to be a minor problem in the inexpensive product case may be considered a glaring and intolerable problem in the expensive product case.

Do you remember that wonderful automobile the Yugo? Basic transportation. The throwaway car. For under $4,000 you could buy what amounted to little more than a go-cart. If you had purchased one, what would have been your expectations about quality? Would you have been upset if the windshield wipers suddenly fell off during a downpour? Would it have bothered you if the window knob that raises and lowers the driver's window suddenly broke off as you were trying to roll up the window during that terrible storm? Both would probably have bothered you, but given the Yugo's price, you probably wouldn't have lost sleep over the incident. On the other hand, instead of a Yugo, lets say you bought a brand new luxury car. What would your expectations be? Chances are, flying windshield wipers and faulty controls would bother you to the point where you might have considered buying something "more reliable."

COSQA Software's customers use price as a weighting factor that affects all the other quality attributes in their quality attributes set. High-priced products receive higher weighting factors while lower-priced products receive lower weighting factors. If they're comparing two products in the same class where one is high priced and the other much lower-priced, they lighten the value they associate with each quality attribute for the lower-priced product. They might purchase the lower-priced product if it possessed all of the elements in their quality attributes set, but since the value they associate with each quality attribute is lower, their expectations about quality would be lower than if they had purchased the higher-priced product. In other words, their expectations about product quality are directly proportional to the price they paid relative to the price of competitive products.

1.2.1.8   Performance

The performance of a product doesn't necessarily refer to how fast or how slow it operates. It can also refer to whether or not the product lives up to customer expectations. How are customer expectations set? In a variety of ways; chief among them is advertising. If the product advertising claims that you can push one thousand transactions per second at a database server with no perceptible system performance degradation, then the system better perform as advertised. If it doesn't, how will their opinion of your product be affected? Most likely, the degree to which it is affected will be a function of the severity of the degradation.

COSQA Software's customers rely upon what they read in industry trade journals and magazines to provide them with accurate information about products that they are considering for purchase. In the past, they have purchased products from companies claiming, through their advertisements, that their products consistently outperform the competition. Occasionally, after purchasing a particular product, they discovered that the performance figures were not as advertised. Feeling deceived in such situations, each made a mental note never to purchase products from that company again.

1.2.2 Organization-Specific Attributes

1.2.2.1   Service and Support

Despite all of your efforts to eliminate defects, make your products easy to use, and deliver top-notch documentation, one of your customers will need help from you directly. They may encounter an installation problem that you did not anticipate, or discover a defect, or they may simply not understand how to invoke or use a particular product feature. Whatever the case, they will turn to you for the answers to their problems. Most customers who call you will expect you to be available and to resolve their problems quickly. If their problems are severe and you are not available or unable to resolve them quickly, you could adversely affect your relationship with that customer. The long-term effect could be that you will lose that customer and possibly all of the prospective customers with whom they share their disappointment.

Customers may consider the quality of your organization before they purchase a product from you. The responsiveness of your service and support organization, the support staff's knowledge and understanding of your product line, their attitude, and their ability to resolve the customer's problems rapidly are all measures of the quality of your organization.

I recently encountered a problem with a certain software vendor's Winsock implementation (Winsock is an application programming interface used to develop client/server applications under the Microsoft Windows family of operating systems). The problem was simple to explain, or so I thought. When I called up the vendor's service and support hotline, I spoke to a representative who had absolutely no knowledge of that particular area of the product. I was on the phone for over an hour describing the problem scenario and the specific steps leading up to the discovery of the problem. The representative was pleasant; however, his lack of knowledge was frustrating me to the point that I almost gave up. I maintained my composure, though and managed to finish my explanation. At the end of our conversation, he told me that I would receive a call within 24 hours from someone who knew more about this area of the product. Well, after waiting two weeks for the call, I decided to change Winsock vendors. My selection of a new vendor was largely influenced by that vendor's service and support reputation.

The customers and prospects of COSQA Software have very high expectations when it comes to service and support. When they call a support organization, they do not want to be greeted by an automated phone system that requires them to listen to endless instructions and press countless buttons before reaching a human being. Finally, they expect the members of a company's support organization to be product experts, not neophytes.

1.2.2.2   Internal Processes

The quality of an organization is also often judged by the processes followed by that organization. Most customers have no idea what ISO 9000 is really all about; however, they ask the question, "Are you registered to ISO 9000?" and often base their decision to purchase your product over another on the basis of whether or not your processes can be described in terms of a "standard" that they trust.

Is it important for you to register to ISO 9000? That depends on whether or not your customers require such registration. Nonetheless, it is important that you follow some reasonable process. You should ask yourself the question, "If my customers were made aware of my processes, what opinion would they hold of my organization?"

While at the C++ World Conference in Austin, Texas, I attended a presentation by the QA manager for Microsoft's Visual C++ Compiler Team. He gave an overview of the processes that they follow to test the Visual C++ Compiler. Prior to attending the conference I had been an avid user of Visual C++, using it to develop test suites for non-GUI applications, the communications subsystems for a backup and recovery product, and for several MFC Windows applications (MFC refers to the Microsoft Foundation Class library used by application developers to develop applications for the Microsoft Windows family of operating systems). I already had a strong opinion about the product. My opinion about the product was based on my personal experiences using the product in ways it was designed to be used. I had opinions about its ease of use, its serviceability, its documentation, and the like. Since I knew nothing about the QA/test processes employed by the Visual C++ team, I often wondered if one day I would suddenly run into a problem with the compiler that would have a profoundly negative impact on my ability to develop my products. When I learned about their processes from its architect, however, my fears were stilled. I was left with a positive feeling about Microsoft and this product. I suddenly felt a high degree of confidence that later releases of the product would serve me equally well.

Most of COSQA Software's customers work for companies that purchase software products only from vendors that have a SEI CMM (SEI stands for Software Engineering Institute and CMM stands for Capability Maturity Model) Level 2 rating. In other words, they will purchase only from vendors whose organizations are ones in which formality prevails. Processes exist and are followed consistently. Sophisticated tools are available and consistently used across the organization. Project schedules, resource requirements, and cost are almost always accurately predicted. Also, they have plans to improve their development processes continuously, with the goal that one day they will achieve the very highest rating: Level 5. Prior to the existence of this policy, COSQA Software's customers often encountered the situation where certain vendors supplied one version of a product with acceptable quality and then followed that version with one of poor quality. Other vendors, however, supplied successive releases of a product with consistently high quality. After examining the development and QA processes of the two types of vendors, they discovered that the vendors that followed documented procedures developed successive releases of products with consistently high quality while the other vendors, following a seat-of-the-pants process, developed successive releases of products with wildly varying and unpredictable degrees of quality. Since the SEI CMM Level 2 rating assured them that a vendor was following a consistent set of processes where predictable results were consistently achieved, they decided to purchase products only from Level 2 rated vendors.

COSQA Software's customer requirements for purchasing software for personal use are not as rigorous as their company's; however, each shares their company's belief that software vendors that continuously improve their development and QA processes and seek an appraisal from recognized agencies consistently produce products of high quality. Though they don't require a specific SEI rating, they speak to vendor "insiders," attend trade shows, and read the trade journals to satisfy their need to know that their vendors are taking steps to assure them that they are developing products of consistently high quality. In the past, they have discontinued personal purchases from vendors that have received bad press about their development and QA processes.

1.3   CONCLUSION

The quality attributes set that we discussed in the preceding sections was presented as an example of a quality attributes set for the customers of a fictitious
software company. Each of your customers, will have
their own set of quality attributes. You must interview
a broad variety of customers asking them to define
quality. From their responses, you will create the quality attributes set that represents their collective definition of quality. The next chapter will present a
processes for carrying out this important step of the QA
program development process.

Keep in mind that the impact that each quality
attribute has on customer opinion of product quality
depends upon the customer. It does not depend on the
value that you personally place on the quality
attribute. Remember that quality is in the eyes of the
beholder. If you will be a customer of the product that
you are creating, then your opinion is as important as
any other. However, don't fall into the trap of counting
your opinion as more valuable than others who may
purchase your product.

Using the quality attributes set discussed above, we
will build a QA program for COSQA Software. Our goal
is to deliver products to COSQA Software's customers
that they will view as having extraordinary quality. As
we progress from section to section and from chapter to
chapter, think of how you can apply what are reading to
your situation. The program that you develop will not
be exactly like the one that we develop in this book
since your customers will have a unique quality
attributes set. The process of developing the program,
however, will be the same.

Chapter 2

Building the Quality Attributes Set

"Listen well"

2.1 INTRODUCTION

The success of a software quality assurance program is ultimately determined by the people who purchase the products produced by that program. Without a thorough understanding of their definition of quality, the success of such a program is left to chance. If luck is on your side, you may develop a software quality assurance program that satisfies their definition without ever asking them for it, but, why leave the success of your program to chance? Why not develop a program whose success can be accurately predicted ahead of time?

Developing such a program is not inherently difficult; however, it requires the engineer to depart from his or her traditional role. Most engineers prefer anonymity and rarely interact with the people who purchase their products. Some companies that I have worked for discourage engineers from talking to customers, fearing that the engineers might reveal some hidden truth about their products that will tarnish the company's reputation. Other's, like BMC Software, Inc., actively encourage their engineers to speak to and interact with their customers to understand their needs better. Understanding your customer's definition of quality, then, requires you to speak directly to them. The best way to communicate is in person; however, since this is not always practical, questionnaires sent through the mail (snail mail or E-mail) work very well. Once you have the customer's ear, what should you ask them? What do you do with the answers they give to your questions? The answers to these questions can be found in the pages of this chapter.

2.2   THE INTERVIEWEE LIST

Recall from Chapter 1 that the quality attributes set is a way to represent customer quality requirements. The first step in the process of building this set is to identify by name the people who will be interviewed. There are two types of people you should interview: customers and prospects. Customers are people who already own products from your company while prospects are people who own none of your products but might someday purchase them. Customers have first-hand experience with your products and possibly products that are similar to yours but from other companies. Prospects have no first-hand experience with your products; however, they may have experience with products similar to yours but from your competitors. Customers are usually the easiest to identify since you may already have their name and address from phone orders or mail-order forms, registration forms, and support calls. Prospects are a little tougher to identify. You may have to enlist the support of a mailing list company or marketing research firm to identify all your prospects by name. If you have a marketing and/or sales department, they may be able help you identify them.

The size of your interviewee list will vary with the size of your market. Certain vertical applications have very small markets while horizontal applications have very large markets. (Vertical applications are designed to meet the needs of a very specific market segment while horizontal applications transcend market segments. For example, applications developed specifically for use by the pharmaceutical industry would be classified as vertical applications while applications developed for use by a large number of different industries would be classified as horizontal applications.) If your list contains a couple dozen names, all of them should be contacted and interviewed in person or by phone (if they are willing, of course!) If your list contains tens of thousands of names, contacting all of them in person or by phone will likely be impossible. For such cases, using a combination of mailed questionnaires, in person interviews, and phone interviews to reach all your candidates can be conducted to achieve accurate results. If your market is made up of people from the same or similar industries all using your products in similar ways, you may want to define a subset of randomly selected interviewees large enough to produce accurate results. For cases where you cannot interview everyone on your interviewee list, the sample size of the subset you choose to interview should be given careful thought. Sample set design is beyond the scope of this book. See *Introduction to the Practice of Statistics* for more information.

2.3 DEVELOP THE QUESTIONNAIRE

Let's take another look at the example quality attributes set from Chapter 1. The elements of the example that comprise the quality attributes set appear in Example 1 at the end of this section for reference. There are three essential components to all quality attributes sets: attribute categories, attribute types, and attribute values. The example has two attribute categories: Product-Specific Attributes and Organization-Specific Attributes. Furthermore, it has eight attribute types listed under the first category and two attribute types under the second. The attribute value assigned to each attribute type is the end result of the process outlined in the remaining sections of this chapter. The attributes set that you develop will likely include the same attribute categories and types as does the example; however, you may want to add additional categories and types to accommodate your own unique situation.

---

[1] David S. Moore and George P. McCabe, *Introduction to the Practice of Statistics*, 2nd ed. (New York: W.H. Freeman and Company, 1993).

Take a close look at the attribute values in Example 1. Notice that they are written using unambiguous and objective language. This facilitates the process of translating these attributes into quality goals and objectives, metrics, and test cases. Thus, questions that you ask your interviewees must be asked in such a way that they elicit an unambiguous and objective response. For example, if you were to ask someone the question, "Is it hot outside today?" they might respond by saying no. Does their answer really tell you whether or not it is hot? It might, if you both have similar tolerances for heat. However, if your tolerance for heat is different, you may discover upon leaving the comfort of your climate controlled office that it is cool outside! A better question to ask would have been, "What is the temperature outside today?" In this case, the respondent must provide an unambiguous, objective response like, "It is 72° outside." The simplest type of response that satisfies these criteria is the yes-no response. Ask your questions so the respondent must answer either yes or no. Also, questions that require the interviewee to select a number from a range satisfy the criteria as well. Not all questions can be asked so the interviewee answers yes or no or selects a number from a range. Don't hesitate to ask such questions but keep in mind that the responses to such questions take considerably longer to pull together to form the quality attributes set.

In addition to the suggestions given above, two important guidelines should be followed while developing a questionnaire:

1. Don't ask leading questions, for example, "You don't mind if the product has a few minor defects, do you?" The implied answer is "no." The interviewee is led to

a particular answer; consequently the validity of all answers to this question would be in doubt. A better question would be, "Would you purchase a product that contains minor defects?" Follow that question with: "Define 'minor defects' and provide several examples of such defects."

2. Don't ask questions that are broad in scope, for example, "Is quality important to you?" If the respondent answers "yes," what would that tell you? It would tell you very little since you don't know their definition of quality!

Now, let's take a look at the questions that COSQA Software designed for its interviewees that ultimately led them to develop the quality attributes set first discussed in Chapter 1 and found in Example 1. Notice the degree to which they did or did not follow the guidelines mentioned above and think of ways they could have improved their questions to achieve optimal results. I encourage you to use their questions as a starting point for the development of your own questionnaire. However, I caution you not to blindly adopt it as a standard for your process. You must take into consideration the uniqueness of your products, your company, and the market to whom you sell your products.

Ease of Use

1. Should a product require the user to consult the user manual to perform basic functions?

2. Should the placement of menus, toolbars, editing windows, status bars, and so on, be similar for all products whether from our company or some other company?

3. Should the function of similarly named menu items and buttons be the same for all products from our company or some other company?

4. Describe the desirable characteristics of a user interface.

5. Describe the undesirable characteristics of a user interface.

Documentation

1. Which is preferable: printed help documentation, online help documentation, or both?

2. Which is preferable: context-sensitive help, searchable help indices, or both?

3. Do you prefer comprehensive voluminous documentation or minimal documentation?

4. Is there a particular type of document that you find indispensable, for example, a quick-start manual, advanced user's guide, and the like?

5. Describe desirable characteristics of product documentation.

6. Describe undesirable characteristics of product documentation.

Defect Tolerance, Frequency, and Impact

1. For each type of defect listed below, specify whether or not you would tolerate such a defect and for how long; the frequency with which you are willing to encounter the defect as you use the product; and its impact on your business.

Defect Type	Tolerate? [Yes/No]	If yes, for how long? [Next release] [Special patch ASAP] [Indefinitely] [N/A]	If yes, how often are you willing to encounter the defect? [Infrequently] [Frequently]	If yes, detrimental impact on your business? [Low] [Moderate] [High]
Some typos in message strings				
Many typos in message strings				
Some typos in on-line help text				
Many typos in on-line help text				
Minor disparities between documented and actual behavior or function				
Major disparities between documented and actual behavior or function				
Application error resulting in an operating system crash				

Defect Type	Tolerate? [Yes/No]	If yes, for how long? [Next release] [Special patch] ASAP] [Indefinitely] [N/A]	If yes, how often are you willing to encounter the defect? [Infrequently] [Frequently]	If yes, detrimental impact on your business? [Low] [Moderate] [High]
Application error resulting in the application terminating				
Application error resulting in an operating system hang				
Application error resulting in the application hanging				
Application error resulting in data corruption				
Short delays between application operations				
Long delays between application operations				

2. Provide an example of a defect that you've encountered that has had a high detrimental impact on your business.

Packaging

1. Do you prefer small, medium, or large product packages? Please include approximate dimensions with your response.

2. Do you prefer light-, medium-, or heavy-weight packages? Please include an approximate weight with your response.

3. Do you prefer colorful, decorative, and informative packaging?

4. Do you look for product endorsements on the package?

5. Do you expect to find a variety of media in the package or is a single media type acceptable?

6. Do you expect to find all product documentation in the package?

7. Please identify anything else that you expect to see on or inside the package?

Price versus Reliability

1. Faced with a decision to purchase a product from one of two vendors where each is equal in function, but one is very inexpensive and of lesser quality and the other is very expensive and of the highest quality, which would you choose?

2. Assuming the same scenario above, but that the products are equal in function and in quality except that the lower-priced product is known to contain

inferior documentation and is poorly packaged, which would you choose?

Performance

1. Is a product's performance relative to competitive products important to you?

2. If so, do you obtain performance information by comparing the products yourself, from the manufacturer's documentation, from product advertisements, or from trade and industry journals?

3. Have you ever purchased a software product advertised to outperform the competition only to discover that it performed poorly in your environment? If so, how did it affect future purchases from that manufacturer?

Service and Support

1. Do you prefer E-mail, fax, automated phone support, or human phone support?

2. How many days per week do you require support?

3. How many hours per day do you require support?

4. How quickly do you expect your problems to be resolved: On the spot, within a few hours of your report, the next business day, within one week, or by the next release?

5. Do you expect support personnel to be highly skilled and experienced engineers, very knowledgeable and experienced users, at least as knowledgeable and experienced as you are, or relatively inexperienced users who follow troubleshooting procedures devel-

oped by more knowledgeable and experienced engineers and users?

Internal Processes

1. Do you prefer to purchase products produced by companies that adhere to formal product development processes and procedures?

2. Do you prefer products produced by companies that have been appraised by an outside organization, such as an accredited appraisal agent of the SEI or ISO? If yes, which level do you prefer?

3. Relate any experiences you have had purchasing products from both companies that have been appraised and those that have not.

Example 1: Quality Attributes Set

Product-Specific Attributes

① Ease of Use

COSQA Software's customers prefer to purchase software products that don't require them to read the manual or use the on-line help facilities. They look for products with Graphical User Interfaces (GUIs) that "look and feel" like other products that they use regularly, such as their word processors and spreadsheet programs. Those programs have what they call "intuitive" user interfaces, which is another way of saying that they can learn the product by playing with it for a short period of time without consulting the manual. They also prefer products that have a GUI that is sparsely populated with buttons and pop-up (or pulldown) menus, leaving a large work area in which they can create their frequent masterpieces.

Product-Specific Attributes (Continued)

② **Documentation**

COSQA Software's customers expect all documentation to be on-line and context sensitive. They also prefer comprehensive and voluminous documentation. They noted that a quick-start or getting-started manual is indispensable. They cannot stand searching through documentation to figure out something as simple as installing the product, invoking it, and using its most elementary features. Also, they find errors in documentation inexcusable. They believe that any product with poorly edited documentation must contain coding errors that will surface someday at a most inopportune moment, destroying one of their works in progress. Fearing such a disaster, they may not purchase a product known to have poorly edited documentation.

③ **Defect Tolerance**

To COSQA Software's customers, defects such as some typos in message strings and in help text as well as minor disparities between documented and actual behavior or function will be tolerated until the next release. On the other hand, they will not tolerate defects that alter or destroy their works in progress or that adversely affect their productivity. Such defects will likely drive them to abandon the product in favor of a product that may be less robust but more reliable. They consider defects such as general exceptions, hangs, data corruption, and long delays between operations to be intolerable defects.

Product-Specific Attributes (Continued)

④ Defect Frequency

Though COSQA Software's customers will tolerate some misspelled words in a product's message strings and help text, they are unwilling to tolerate large numbers of misspelled words or typos. Minor defects that appear frequently end up distracting or frustrating them to the point that their productivity suffers and they consider anything that adversely affects their productivity to be an intolerable major defect.

⑤ Defect Impact

COSQA Software's customers see themselves as highly productive people who prefer to work on several things at once. They often start several applications on their workstations simultaneously, jumping from one to another. Many of COSQA Software's customers have had an experience where they noticed that whenever they jumped from their word processor to a particular vendor's desktop publishing system, they have had to wait several minutes for the view to redraw. The desktop publishing system developers decided to optimize memory usage, thereby sacrificing view redrawing performance. They assumed that most users would not switch from application to application while using their product; consequently view redrawing would be infrequent. To save memory, they decided to save the current view on disk, retrieving it whenever they needed to perform a redraw. This design decision saved a large amount of memory but sacrificed redrawing performance. Though some users might appreciate the designers' effort to decrease memory usage, COSQA Software's customers viewed the resulting poor performance of view redrawing as a major defect since it severely impacted their productivity.

Product-Specific Attributes (Continued)

⑥ **Packaging**

The customers who were interviewed for COSQA Software's new product believe that quality software products are found only in large packages having substantial weight, that are covered with colorful award winning graphic designs and descriptions of the product's features in excruciating detail, and that are emblazoned with endorsements from the leading trade magazines. The box must be filled to capacity with floppies or CD-ROMs, lots of documentation, and offers for free demo software.

⑦ **Price versus Reliability**

COSQA Software's customers use price as a weighting factor that affects all the other quality attributes in their quality attributes sets. High-priced products receive higher weighting factors while lower-priced products receive lower weighting factors. If they're comparing two products in the same class where one is high priced and the other much lower-priced, they lighten the value they associate with each quality attribute for the lower-priced product. They might purchase the lower-priced product if it possessed all of the elements in their quality attributes set, but since the value they associate with each quality attribute is lower, their expectations about quality would be lower than if they had purchased the higher-priced product. In other words, their expectations about product quality are directly proportional to the price they paid relative to the price of competitive products.

Product-Specific Attributes (Continued)

---

⑧ Performance

COSQA Software's customers rely upon what they read in industry trade journals and magazines to provide them with accurate information about products that they are considering for purchase. In the past, they have purchased products from companies claiming, through their advertisements, that their products consistently outperform the competition. Occasionally, after purchasing a particular product, they have discovered that the performance figures were not as advertised. Feeling deceived in such situations, each made a mental note never to purchase products from that company again.

Organization-Specific Attributes

---

⑨ Service and Support

The customers and prospects of COSQA Software have very high expectations when it comes to service and support. When they call a support organization, they do not want to be greeted by an automated phone system that requires them to listen to endless instructions and press countless buttons before reaching a human being. Finally, they expect the members of a company's support organization to be product experts, not neophytes.

Organization-Specific Attributes (Continued)

⑩ **Internal Processes**

Most of COSQA Software's customers work for companies that purchase software products only from vendors that have a SEI CMM Level 2 rating. In other words, their companies will purchase only from vendors whose organizations are ones in which formality prevails. Processes exist and are followed consistently. Sophisticated tools are available and consistently used across an organization. Project schedules, resource requirements, and cost are almost always accurately predicted. Also, they must have plans to one day achieve the very highest rating; Level 5. Prior to the existence of this policy, COSQA Software's customers often encountered the situation where certain vendors supplied one version of a product with acceptable quality and then followed that version with one of poor quality. Other vendors, however, supplied successive releases of a product with consistently high quality. After examining the development and QA processes of the two types of vendors, they discovered that the vendors that followed documented procedures developed successive releases of products with consistently high quality while the other vendors, following a seat-of-the-pants process, developed successive releases of products with wildly varying and unpredictable degrees of quality. Since the SEI CMM Level 2 rating assured them that a vendor was following documented processes, they decided to purchase products only from Level 2 rated vendors.

Organization-Specific Attributes (Continued)

COSQA Software's customer requirements for purchasing software for personal use are not as rigorous as their company's; however, each shares their company's belief that software vendors that continuously improve their development and QA processes and seek an appraisal from recognized agencies consistently produce products of high quality. Though they don't require a specific SEI rating, they speak to vendor "insiders," attend trade shows, and read the trade journals to satisfy their need to know that their vendors are taking steps to assure them that they are developing products of consistently high quality. In the past, they have discontinued personal purchases from vendors that have received bad press about their development and QA processes.

2.4   BUILD A QUALITY ATTRIBUTES SET FOR EACH INTERVIEWEE

Now that you know whom you are going to interview and what you are going to ask them, it is time to conduct the interview and build an attributes sets for each. As mentioned earlier in this chapter, the interviewees can be interviewed in one of three ways: in person, by telephone, and by mail (snail mail or E-mail). The best method is to speak to interviewees in person since it gives you an opportunity to consider their body language and facial expressions as they respond to your questions. It also allows you to establish a personal relationship with them. The benefits of such a relationship can be enormous, particularly if you establish a positive rapport. Once you've established a positive rapport, they will be more inclined to tell you what they really think. Make your interviewees feel that you really care about them and their needs. The next best method is by telephone for reasons similar to those given for the "in-person" method with the exception that you will not have an opportunity to consider body language in their responses. The final method is by mail. It has one particular advantage that the others do not. It allows you to reach a large number of interviewees rather efficiently. Unfortunately, though, most of them will not return the questionnaire. Also, since the randomness of the respondents cannot be guaranteed, it will be difficult to determine if the respondents represent a reasonable subset of your prospective interviewees. If you use the final method, be certain to interview a random sample from the interviewee list in person and by phone to see if their responses fall within the range of responses from those who were interviewed by mail—an informal way to test the validity of the sample.

For both the "in-person" and "by-telephone" methods, be certain to ask the interviewees if they have time to answer your questions. Also, tell them how long it will take to conduct the interview. If you are offering them an incentive, you may want to open the conversation with, "Hello, my name is Frank from COSQA Software Corporation. I am conducting a quality assurance review for my company so we may serve you better in the future. If you have approximately 20 minutes to spare, I would like to ask you several questions. We are offering a 25 percent discount to all interviewees." If they say no, they're not interested, then thank them and leave (or hang up). You may also ask them if they know of anyone who may be interested in participating. If they say that they don't have the time right now, ask them if you can call back at another time. If they say yes, then do so and conduct the interview. During the interview, avoid chit-chat. Stick to the questions and work through your list as quickly and as efficiently as possible without appearing to rush. If they want to talk at length about some item, make a note on your interview form and ask them politely if they would mind waiting until after all questions have been asked before discussing any item at length. Then, when you have finished asking all of your questions, return to the marked items. If an interviewee is not responding with the unambiguous, objective, and quantifiable answers that your questions are designed to elicit, then ask them to be more specific. For example, if an interviewee were to respond to Question 1 under Ease of Use above by saying, "I really don't like to read user manuals," ask them to explain why. They may say, "Every user manual I've ever read is so boring that I can't stand to look at another." You may want to rephrase your question to this interviewee by asking, "If the user manuals were interesting, should a product require the user to consult the user manual to perform basic functions?" Sometimes, it is necessary to rephrase a question, on the fly, to achieve the desired result of eliciting an unambiguous, quantifiable, and objective answer. This brings up another important reason to conduct at least some of your interviews in person and by telephone: to test your questionnaire. If you find yourself rephrasing a particular question often, it is a good signal that the question should be reworded.

The "by-mail" method involves much less effort up front on your part, unless of course, you must personally label and stuff each envelope with a questionnaire and self-addressed stamped return envelope. If possible, send your questionnaires via E-mail. It will save you an enormous amount of upfront time. The bulk of the effort for this method comes later when you must sort through each response. The value of a well-designed questionnaire becomes apparent when using this method. If poorly designed, you may get answers that make no sense, are ambiguous, unobjective, and perhaps unquantifiable. For all three methods, the responses collected for each interviewee represent the quality attributes set for that person. In the next section, we'll examine ways to pull together and reduce this potentially large set of responses to create the quality attributes set that represents their collective definition of quality.

Our fictitious software company, COSQA Software, conducted their interviews using a combination of all three interview methods. Prior to developing the question set, they identified over 10,000 interviewee candidates by name and address. The first 3,000 were customers whose names and addresses were taken from registration forms and service and support logs. The names and addresses for the remaining 7,000 interviewee candidates were purchased from a mailing list company that was able to provide COSQA Software with the names and addresses of people who had recently purchased products from their competition. From the list they selected at random 100 candidates to interview by telephone, 10 to interview in person, and sent the remaining 9,890 prospective interviewees a copy of the questionnaire along with a self-addressed stamped returned envelope (they didn't want the interviewee candidates to have an excuse not to send back the questionnaire!). As an incentive to answer the questionnaire, they offered all respondents a 25 percent discount on the next release of their flagship product.

At this point you may be saying to yourself, "This seems as if it would take quite a bit of my time. I don't think I have the time to spare!" Or perhaps, "COSQA Software must have an army of employees that have nothing better to do than talk on the phone and mail letters!" If the market for your product is large and the composition varied, deploying a massive interviewing campaign may be infeasible. Instead, you may decide to implement such a campaign on a much smaller scale. On the other hand, you may have the necessary time and human resources to deploy a comprehensive interview campaign. The accuracy of your results ultimately depends on the completeness of your interviewee list, the size of your sample, and the quality of the questions that you ask. If your interviewee list is incomplete, your sample too small, or questions poor, your results may not be reliable.

2.5   THE QUALITY ATTRIBUTES SETS

With the interviews behind you comes the task of taking all of your interviewees' responses and pulling them together to form the quality attributes set. The complexity of this task is directly related to the number of responses you received as well as the types of questions that you asked. For example, if all of your questions elicited yes-no or range responses, then the task of pulling the responses together is straightforward. In fact, the process can be automated by using scannable interview forms. On the other hand, if your questions elicited lengthy responses, the process of pulling the answers together can be very time consuming and error prone.

The questions on our sample questionnaire consist primarily of those that have yes-no and range responses; however, several questions require the interviewee to respond with a textual response. We start the process of pulling the answers together by tallying up responses to yes-no and range response questions and recording the number of each response on a blank questionnaire that I'll refer to as the consolidated questionnaire. Then, we examine each textual response, looking for words that capture the essence of the interviewee's response. For example, Question 6 under Ease of Use on the sample questionnaire asks, "Describe the desirable characteristics of a user interface." A typical response might be, "I like an interface that has lots of buttons with bitmaps on them that indicate what they do. I really hate to use pop-up menus. I also like context-sensitive help. It really makes it easy to figure out how to do something when you have context-sensitive help!" What are the essential elements of what this interviewee is saying? Looking at the response, we know he "likes self-descriptive buttons," "dislikes pop-up menus," and "likes context-sensitive help." Record each of these essential elements under this question on the consolidated questionnaire. Later, after all responses are recorded in this fashion, go through the responses and tally up the number of like responses.

The final step in the process of creating the union of quality attributes sets is to describe, in unambiguous, objective, and quantifiable terms, the quality attributes set that represents your customers' definition of quality. Six questions were asked under Ease of Use on the sample questionnaire. After tallying up responses, the following distribution of answers was collected:

Ease of Use

1. Should a product require the user to consult the user manual to perform basic functions?

   Yes (50) No (9750) Unimportant (200)

2. Should the placement of menus, toolbars, editing windows, status bars, and the like, be similar for all products whether from our company or some other company?

   Yes (9750) No (50) Unimportant (200)

3. Should the function of similarly named menu items and buttons be the same for all products from our company or some other company?

   Yes (9750) No (50) Unimportant (200)

4. Describe the desirable characteristics of a user interface.

   "likes self-descriptive buttons" (4025)

   "dislikes pop-up menus" (8625)

   "likes context-sensitive help" (9725)

Based on this distribution of responses, the following attribute value was assigned to the "Ease of Use" attribute type:

COSQA Software's customers prefer to purchase software products that don't require them to read the manual or use the on-line help facilities. When they need help, however, they prefer to use on-line help rather than printed manuals. They also prefer products that have a Graphical User Interface (GUI) that is sparsely populated with buttons and pop-up (or pull-down) menus. They look for products with GUIs that "look and feel" like products that they use from other companies.

Notice that the attribute value in this example accounts for only the most-often given responses. In other words, the least-often given responses have been thrown out! Is that wise? After all, by throwing out responses, aren't we running the risk of alienating those customers? Possibly, however, it is not always possible for you to satisfy everyone's requirements. You must take a look at the cost associated with satisfying a few "special" customers versus the potential return. For example, let's suppose that COSQA Software decided to satisfy the 25 customers who prefer printed manuals rather than on-line help in our example. Does reducing profit margins to accommodate 25 customers out of 10,000 outweigh the need to keep their business? That's not always an easy question to answer since those 25 customers may represent a significant portion of your business in the future. No easy answer can be given here. You must carefully weigh the costs associated with trying to satisfy every customer's requirements versus the return. Our fictitious software company, COSQA Software, chose to throw out the least-given responses.

The remaining attribute values, listed in Example 1, were similary derived. It is left as an exercise for the reader to deduce the consolidated responses to the questionnaire based on the attribute values listed in Example 1.

2.6 CONCLUSION

Building the quality attributes set requires the engineer to depart from his or her traditional role to speak directly to the customer to determine their quality requirements. The process of developing the quality attributes set begins by identifying all of the customers and prospective customers who make up the market. Once identified, a questionnaire is developed to ask them questions designed to elicit unambiguous, objective, and quantifiable responses to questions under each quality attribute type. With responses in hand, results are tallied and a value assigned to each quality attribute type. The result is the quality attributes set that describes customer quality requirements.

The final step in the process is not always easy since you will often be faced with deciding whether or not you should accommodate the requirements of all the customers and prospects that exist within your market. If you decide not to accommodate the needs of some of them, then be certain that their business short term and near term is not valuable. You might be pushing away customers that in the long run may prove to be your largest.

Chapter 3

Quality Metrics

3.1 INTRODUCTION

The quality attributes set represents customer quality requirements. Once defined, this information is used to help us answer two of the most important product development questions: During the development process, *will we* produce a product that meets or exceeds these requirements, and at the end of the development process, *have we* produced a product that meets or exceeds them? The first question must be asked repeatedly throughout the development process. When the answer to the question is negative, adjustments must be made to the process to bring the project back on course. Positive answers reassure us that we are heading toward our goal to produce a product that meets or exceeds customer quality requirements. The second question is asked at the end as a final check, to make sure that a product was produced that will satisfy the customer. If the first question is asked often enough and solicits answers that provide conclusive evidence that we are heading toward our goal, the question asked at the end should readily confirm that an acceptable product has been produced.

Literally asking the question, "Are we building or have we built something that will ultimately meet or exceed customer requirements?" throughout the development process or at its conclusion will not provide us with the conclusive evidence that we seek, however. Imagine for a moment that you are a physician (indeed, you may be!) in an emergency room and a patient is brought to you for treatment. You ask your patient, "How are you feeling?" They reply, "Terrible!" Could you offer a treatment at that point? Not likely. To diagnose their condition accurately, you would perform specific tests, such as measure their heart rate, blood pressure, and temperature. You might perform a series of tests designed to help you determine accurately the cause of their condition. You would then compare the results with what are considered "normal" results. Anything that falls outside of this "normal" range will likely point to the cause of their malady. Once you have determined what is ailing them, you would prescribe a course of treatment. Hopefully, assuming that you ran the right tests, received accurate results, and prescribed the proper course of treatment, the patient will recover. To make sure that the patient is getting better, you would monitor their progress by repeatedly applying tests and comparing them to the desired results. If your patient's condition began to drift away from the desired results, you would alter the treatment until you could see a trend leading toward the desired results.

The role of the quality assurance engineer is not unlike that of the physician. For each element of the customer quality attributes set, you must select and possibly create specific measurements that can be applied repeatedly during the development process and then again at its conclusion. The results of such measurements can be used to determine progress toward and finally attainment of quality goals.

In the preceding analogy, notice that as a physician you must compare the results of your diagnostic tests to some set of "normal" results. Based on deviations from "normal," you can determine the cause of your patient's illness. The test results alone tell you nothing about the condition of your patient. As a quality assurance engineer, the results of the measurements that you take will not allow you to judge the quality of your product. You must compare your results to some set of desirable values. Measurements combined with desired results are referred to as metrics. Metrics alone are not the only method available to us to perform such an evaluation. In our analogy, you could ask the patient specific questions such as, "Where does it hurt?" to assist you in making a proper diagnosis. In fact, asking your patient questions may be the only way to determine what ails them. As a quality assurance engineer, it may be both desirable and necessary to ask questions in addition to applying metrics throughout the development and test process. In addition, physicians as well as quality assurance engineers can use checklists as an appraisal tool.

   There are two goals for this chapter: Develop an understanding of and appreciation for metrics and other methods of analysis and to define a process that can be followed to build a set of specific metrics from a quality attributes set. We will develop such a set for the customers of our fictitious software company, COSQA Software. In a later chapter we will learn how to use it to guide the development and test process toward attainment of our ultimate goal: Produce a product that meets or exceeds customer requirements.

3.2   TYPES OF METRICS

In his book *Metrics and Models in Software Quality Engineering*,[1] Stephen H. Kan refers to three different types of software metrics: process, product, and project. According to Kan, process metrics can be used to improve the software development and maintenance process. Metrics such as *effectiveness of defect removal during development, pattern of testing defect arrival*, and *response time of the fix process* are listed as examples. Product metrics describe the characteristics of the product, such as *its size, complexity, performance*. Finally, project metrics describe the characteristics of the project and its execution, such as *number of software developers, staffing pattern over the life-cycle of the product, cost, and schedule*. Kan, goes on to define software quality metrics as the subset of software metrics that focuses on the quality aspects of the process, product, and project. He then further divides software quality metrics into in-process and end-product quality metrics and then states:

> The essence of software quality engineering is to investigate the relationships among in-process metrics, project characteristics, and end-product quality; and, based on the findings, to engineer improvements in both process and product quality.

As part of his discussion on product quality metrics, Kan introduces the customer stating that good software quality engineering practice needs to consider the customer's perspective. Like other texts on the subject of quality assurance, Kan believes that quality improvement should be driven by the development team. The essential difference between customer-oriented software quality assurance and methodologies like Kan's is that quality improvements are driven by the customer.

Customer-oriented software quality assurance divides software quality metrics into two categories: process and product. The metrics that are developed or selected for the production and maintenance of a product are determined by customer requirements as embodied by the quality attributes set. By placing customer requirements ahead of internal requirements, and by involving the customer from the beginning of the development process, through delivery, and during maintenance, you maximize your ability to produce a product that will satisfy their quality requirements. If

---

[1] Stephen H. V, *Metrics and Models in Software Quality Engineering* (Reading, MA: Addison-Wesley Publishing Company, 1995), pp. 83–84.

you ignore your customers until you have finished with
development or you wait until after the product is
released, you will likely produce something that falls
short of satisfying their requirements. Place them first,
involve them every step of the way, let them know that
you are placing their interests ahead of yours and you
will not only produce a product that satisfies them; you
will also gain a devoted customer.

3.3   THE METRICS BUCKET

The quality attributes set for your customers will drive
the metrics selection and development process detailed
in an upcoming section. Before discussing this process,
however, it is worthwhile to review some of the more
common software quality metrics in use today. For your
particular application, you may select only one, possibly two, all, or none of the metrics listed! Keep in mind
that there are two components to a metric: the measurement itself, and the acceptable value or values
associated with that metric. In most cases, you will
choose to define only the measurement portion of a metric and select the acceptable value or values for that
metric by asking your customers what they should be.

The metrics listed in the next two sections are
divided into both process metrics and product metrics.
Process metrics are applied to the production and
maintenance processes while product metrics are
applied to the product during the various stages of
those processes. Some authors further divide metric
types by process stage and suggest that readers apply
them during the particular stage under which they are
classified. This division works for organizations that

organize by function; however, for organizations that integrate the various functions and follow less traditional process methodologies, such a division is meaningless. We will explore this particular topic in depth in Chapter 5.

3.3.1 Process Metrics

3.3.1.1   Defect arrival rate

A very useful process metric is the *defect arrival rate*. It is the number of defects found during testing measured at regular intervals over some period of time. Rather than a single value, a set of values is associated with this metric. When plotted on a graph, the data may rise, indicating a positive *defect arrival rate*; it may stay flat, indicating a constant *defect arrival rate*; or decrease, indicating a negative *defect arrival rate*.

Interpretation of the results of this metric can be very difficult, however. Intuitively, one might interpret a negative defect arrival rate to indicate that the product is improving since the number of new defects found is declining over time. To validate this interpretation, you must eliminate certain possible causes for the decline. For example, it could be that *test effectiveness* is declining over time. In other words, the tests may only be effective at uncovering certain types of problems. Once those problems have been found, the tests are no longer effective since they have already found the problems that they were designed to find and were unable to uncover other types of problems. Unless new tests are developed to cover areas previously left untested, the decline in *test effectiveness* would manifest itself as a decline in the defect arrival rate. Another possibility is that the test organization is understaffed and consequently is unable to adequately test the product between measurement intervals. They focus their efforts during the first interval on performing stress tests that expose many problems, followed by executing system tests during the next interval where fewer problems are uncovered, and ending with the execution of component tests that find even fewer problems during the next measurement interval. A plot of the defect arrival rate over the time span of three measurement intervals might suggest that the product is improving when, in fact, it tells very little about the state of product quality.

It is important to remember for each metric chosen or developed that the value generated as a result of the measurement taken does not give a complete picture of reality. You must interpret the meaning behind a particular result within the context of the process and the results of the other measurements.

3.3.1.2   Test effectiveness

Tests that always pass are considered ineffective. This does not mean that you should not execute tests that never find defects! Such tests form what are known as regression tests. If any of them ever fail, a regression in the product's quality has occurred. To measure *test effectiveness* (TE), take the number of defects found by formal tests (D_n) and divide by the total number of formal tests (T_n):

$$TE = D_n / T_n$$

When calculated at regular intervals and plotted, *test effectiveness* can be observed over some period of time. If the graph rises over time, *test effectiveness* may be improving. On the other hand, if the graph is falling over time, *test effectiveness* may be waning. Like the last metric, interpretation of the results must be made within the context of the process that you are following and the results of the other measurements.

3.3.1.3   Defects by phase

Anyone who has calculated the cost of repairing a defect in a product that has been deployed versus eliminating the defect in the earliest phases of the development process will tell you that it is much less expensive in terms of resources and reputation to eliminate early instead of fix late. The *defects by phase* metric is a variation of the *defect arrival rate* metric. Rather then take a count of the new defects that have arrived during some regular time interval, the domain of this function is the development phase. At the conclusion of each discreet phase of the development process, a count of the new defects is taken and plotted to observe a trend. If the graph appears to be rising, you might infer that the methods used for defect detection and removal during the earlier phases are not effective since the rate at which new defects are being discovered is increasing. On the other hand, if the graph appears to be falling, you might conclude that early defect detection and removal is effective.

As an example, consider the company that followed a traditional five-phase development process: requirements analysis, high-level design, low-level design, implementation, and test phases to build a new product. In a mad rush to market, the managers decided to bypass their formal review and inspection processes, believing that their highly skilled and talented staff of programmers would catch anything awry while writing the code! During requirements analysis, several defects were uncovered and logged. But, since a formal review was not performed, many defects remained hidden from sight. During high-level design several more defects were discovered. In fact, several contradicting requirements were discovered that were overlooked during the previous phase.

Management began to get anxious at this point: "Why aren't you coding yet?" The engineers, feeling pressure to move on, hurried through the low-level design, arguing that they could design and code at the same time! As they began coding they uncovered even more requirements-related defects and discovered a major architectural flaw. Pressing forward though, they managed to put together something that resembled the product they had set out to create. Now it was time to test the product.

Under test, the product fell apart. Major inconsistencies between requirements and implementation were uncovered. Every time the product failed a test, arguments ensued between the development and test engineers. The test engineers claimed the product had a defect while the development engineers claimed that the tests were written incorrectly. Every time a fix was applied to the system, three new problems appeared! Looking at the plot of the *defects by phase* metric, it was obvious that there was a major problem with the process. By pushing defect detection and removal to the end of the process, the management team had set itself up for failure. If they had established a *defects by phase* metric that required a declining new defect count over phases, they would then have seen early on that they were destined to fail. At that point, they could have adjusted their process by reinstituting the formal review and inspection processes that they had bypassed.

Though the preceding account is not from an actual case study, such scenarios are all too common. When chosen properly, metrics can help an organization identify the weaknesses in its processes. Once identified, corrective action can be taken.

3.3.1.4   Defect removal effectiveness

Defect removal effectiveness (DRE) can be calculated by dividing the number of defects removed prior to release (D_r) by the sum of defects removed prior to release (D_r) and the total number of defects that remain in the product at release (D_t). When multiplied by 100, this value can be expressed as a percentage:

$$DRE = D_r / (D_r + D_t)$$

How do you determine the total number of defects that remain in the product? Statistical methods can be applied to determine the number of defects that remain or a simple count of known unresolved defects can be used. For the sake of simplicity, a simple count of remaining defects will suffice. When calculated this way, however, the accuracy of this metric is dependent on the thoroughness of your testing and diligence with which your staff reports defects.

If you follow a phased development process, this metric can be applied on a phase-by-phase basis. By plotting percent effectiveness versus phase, you can compare the relative effectiveness of defect removal by phase. Using this information, weak areas in your process can be targeted for improvement during subsequent development cycles. When applying the metric in this way, *defect removal effectiveness* is calculated by dividing the number of defects removed during a phase by the sum of the total number of defects removed during that phase and the number of defects that remain in the product at the end of that phase. Again, the accuracy of this metric is dependent on the thoroughness of your testing and diligence with which your staff reports defects. When plotted by phase, a *defect removal effectiveness* trend can be observed and, if necessary, used to adjust the development process.

3.3.1.5   Defect backlog

In its simplest form, the *defect backlog* metric is a count of the number of defects in the product following its release. It is usually measured at regular intervals of time and plotted for trend analysis. By itself, this metric provides very little useful information. For example, what does a *defect backlog* count of 128 tell you? Can you predict the impact of those defects on customers? Can you estimate the time it would take to repair those defects? Can you recommend changes to improve the development process?

A more useful way to represent the *defect backlog* is by defect severity. Assume for a moment that your company uses four different severity levels where severity level 4 is a minor enhancement request that has little, if no, impact on your customer's business operations and severity level 1 is a major defect that halts their business operations. By calculating the *defect backlog* by severity level, you can begin to draw useful conclusions from your measurements. For example, a month after the initial release of your product, the backlog contains 2 severity 1 defects, 8 severity 2 defects, 28 severity 3 defects, and 90 severity 4 defects. Based on this information, you might shift resources to quickly resolve the severity 1 and 2 defects. Since there are such a large number of enhancement requests, you may take a closer look at how you gather requirements.

3.3.1.6 Backlog management index

Unfortunately, and despite your best efforts to carefully gather requirements, design, implement, and test your product, problems will arise after your product is released. As the backlog is worked, new problems arrive that impact the net result of your team's efforts to reduce the backlog. If the number of new defects exceeds the number of defects closed over some period of time, your team is losing ground to the backlog. If, on the other hand, your team closes problems faster than new ones are opened, they are gaining ground. The *backlog management index* (BMI) is calculated by dividing the number of defects closed during some period of time (D_c) by the number of new defects that arrived during that same period of time (D_n).

$$BMI = D_c / D_n$$

If the result is greater than 1, your team is gaining ground; otherwise it is losing. When measurements are taken at regular intervals and plotted, a trend can be observed indicating the rate at which the backlog is growing or shrinking.

3.3.1.7   Fix response time

The *fix response time* metric is determined by calculating the average time it takes your team to fix a defect. The time it takes to fix a defect can be measured several different ways. In some cases, it is the elapsed time between the discovery of the defect and the development of an unverified fix. In other cases, it is the elapsed time between the discovery and the development of a verified fix.

Like the *defect backlog* metric, by itself, this metric provides very little useful information. A better alternative is to measure *fix response time* by severity. Since severe defects typically interfere with a customer's business operations, a fast *fix response time* is key to maintaining customer satisfaction. On the other hand, minor defects typically call for a much less demanding *fix response time*.

3.3.1.8   Percent delinquent fixes

A fix is delinquent if it exceeds your *fix response time* criteria. In other words, if you have established a maximum *fix response time* of 48 hours; then *fix response times* that exceed 48 hours are considered delinquent. To calculate the *percent delinquent fixes* (PDF); divide the number of delinquent fixes (F_d) by the number of nondelinquent fixes (F_n) and multiply by 100.

$$PDF = (F_d \, / \, F_n) * 100$$

This metric is also measured better by severity since the consequences of having a high *percent delinquent fixes* for severe defects is typically much greater than for less severe or minor defects.

3.3.1.9   Defective fixes

A defect for which a fix has been prepared that later turns out to be defective or worse, creates one or more additional problems, is called a defective fix. The *defective fixes* metric is a count of the number of such fixes. To accurately measure the number of defective fixes, your organization must not only keep track of defects that have been closed and then reopened but must also keep track of new defects that were caused by a defect fix.

3.3.2   Product Metrics

3.3.2.1   Defect density

The *defect density* metric is used to measure the number of defects discovered per some unit of product size (usually KLOC or Thousand of Lines of Code.) For example, if your product has 10 KLOC and 127 defects were discovered during a test cycle, the *defect density* would be 0.0127 defects per KLOC. Is this good or bad? That depends on your customers. Should you ask your customers, "How many defects per KLOC are you willing to accept?" No! They probably will not have any idea what you are asking. However, studies have shown that if a product is found to have a large number of defects during formal testing, customers will discover a similarly large number of defects while using the product.

Conversely, if a small number of defects are found during formal testing, a small number of defects will be found by customers. When building the quality attributes set for your customers, questions that relate to their tolerance of defects can help you select an acceptable value for this metric. Some corporations use a value known as six sigma for this metric which is 3.4 defects per million lines of code!

Hopefully, at some point in your development process, you perform some form of testing. The type of testing performed could be unit testing, integration testing, system testing, field testing, and so on. The timing and frequency with which you perform testing depends on the type of development process that you follow. Some organizations follow a process where testing occurs after all development work has been completed. Other organizations follow a similar process but perform unit testing during development; integration testing once the various system components have been pulled together; system testing usually follows, and then field testing is performed. Still other organizations follow a process like the latter but incrementally build and integrate, producing several intermediate versions of the product. The defect density metric can be applied during any test period; however, only the value calculated during test phases that follow system integration can be used to make predictions about the rate at which defects will be discovered by customers.

3.3.2.2   Defects by severity

The *defects by severity* metric is a simple count of the number of unresolved defects listed by severity. Typically, this metric is measured at some regular interval and plotted to determine whether or not a trend exists. Ideally, a trend exists, showing progress toward the acceptable values for each severity. Movement away from those values should raise a flag that the project is at risk of failing to satisfy the conditions of the metric.

3.3.2.3   Mean time between failure

The *mean time between failure* (MTBF) metric is a simple average of the elapsed time between failures that occur during testing. For example, if your product is being tested for a period of 48 hours and failures are encountered at 15 hours elapsed time, 28 hours elapsed time, and 48 hours elapsed time, MTBF is calculated by adding the times between the failures, 15, 13, and 20, and then dividing by 3.

Typically, this metric is defined in terms of the type of testing performed during the measurement period. For example, MTBF during moderate-stress testing is distinguished from MTBF during heavy-stress testing. As you will see later, the type of testing performed to calculate MTBF will depend on customer quality requirements as defined by the quality attributes set. If your customers never heavily stress the product, MTBF should be calculated under conditions of less-than-heavy stress. Does that mean that you should not set an MTBF for the case where the product is heavily stressed? No, in fact, pushing the system beyond its limits is a useful way to flush out some of the more subtle defects. In this scenario, however, the less-than-heavy stress version of MTBF is a minimum ship criteria and the heavy-stress version of MTBF is set to push the product's quality beyond expectations.

3.3.2.4   Customer-reported problems

The *customer-reported problems* metric is a simple count of the number of new (nonduplicate) problems reported by customers over some time interval. When measured at regular time intervals and plotted, the data can be used to identify a trend. Although a trend may be apparent, it is more useful to determine the reasons behind the trend.

If, for example, the number of *customer-reported problems* increases over time, is it because more end users are using the product? If you measure the number of customers who use the product at the same intervals that you measure *customer-reported problems*, you might identify a cause-effect or correlation between the metric and number of end users. For example, if you determine that as the number of end users of the system increases the number of customer-reported problems increases, a relationship may exist between the two that suggests that you may have a serious scalability flaw in your product.

On the other hand, is the increase related to greater demands placed on the system by end users as their experience with the product matures? If you implement your product with a profiling feature, you can monitor how your customers use the product, that is, which functions they use and how often, what kind of load they place on the system, and so forth. If you measure profiling information at the same interval as *customer-reported problems*, you might identify a cause-effect or correlation between the metric and end-user usage or load. For example, if you determine that as load increases the number of *customer-reported problems* increases, a relationship may exist between the two that suggests that you may have a serious load capacity flaw in your product.

3.3.2.5   Customer satisfaction

The *customer satisfaction* metric is typically measured through a customer satisfaction survey. In such a survey, a number of questions are asked from one or more categories. Answers are usually in the form of range-response, that is, questions are answered by selecting a number from 1 to 5 where 1 represents a very negative response and 5 represents a very positive response. Finally, the data are summarized.

Minimally, questions should be designed to assess both the respondent's subjective, as well as objective perceptions of product quality. For example, a survey might ask the question: "On a scale from 1 to 5 where 1 is poor and 5 is outstanding, rate the overall quality of the product." Clearly, this is a very subjective question. On the other hand, an example of an objective question is: "Since you have deployed the product in your production environment, has the number of defects that you have encountered in the product exceeded your pre-defined defect limit?"

3.4   BEYOND METRICS

Metrics provide us with a means to determine whether or not a product satisfies some set of requirements. Do metrics always suffice? Can metrics be selected from the bucket, or designed, that allow you to determine whether or not your product satisfies your customers' quality requirements as expressed by their quality attributes set? Not always. For example, which metric from the bucket (my bucket or yours) would allow you to determine whether or not you are satisfying the documentation-related quality attribute from the quality attributes set for COSQA Software's customers?

COSQA Software's customers expect all documentation to be on-line and context sensitive. They also prefer comprehensive and voluminous documentation. They noted that a quickstart or getting-started manual is indispensable. They cannot stand searching through documentation to figure out something as simple as installing the product, invoking it, and using its most elementary features. Also, they find errors in documentation inexcusable. They believe that any product with poorly edited documentation must contain coding errors that will someday surface at a most inopportune moment destroying one of their works in progress. Fearing such a disaster, they may not purchase a product known to have poorly edited documentation.

Certain elements of the attribute above are obvious candidates for metrics. For example, "they find errors in documentation inexcusable" is a candidate for a *defect backlog* metric where the acceptable value of the metric is 0. However, what metric can be used to determine whether or not a quick start manual exists or whether or not the documentation is on-line and context sensitive? Further, how does one determine whether or not the product possesses a particular element of an attribute that is wholly subjective? For example,

COSQA Software's customers' quality attributes set specifies:

> Those programs have what they call "intuitive" user interfaces, which is another way of saying that they can learn the product by playing with it for a short period of time without consulting the manual.

For such elements of an attribute, other means should be used to track whether or not the product possesses the attribute including usability studies and checklists.

3.4.1 Usability Studies

Typically, usability studies are conducted by independent test labs that invite groups of end users to their test facility to evaluate the usability of a product. Selection of the participants is critical to the success of such studies. For example, if a product is a specialized tool like a visual compiler, the invitees should be software developers who both regularly use visual compilers and have been exposed to a variety of such tools. If a product is a general-purpose tool like a word processor, the participants should be drawn from a much larger group of people including technicians, managers, administrative assistants, and executives from various trades and industries.

In addition to selecting and inviting an appropriate group of end users, a script is typically developed. This script directs the participants to perform various tasks. Following the completion of each task, they are asked to record their experience. For example, a word processor usability study might ask the participants to underline a passage of text without consulting the user documentation and then comment on the difficulty of the task. Or, it may ask the participants to develop a three-column multipage newsletter using on-line documentation. Again, following the completion of the task, the participants are asked to comment on its difficulty.

A usability study is an effective means by which to determine whether or not a product satisfies the various subjective attributes and attribute elements of a usability attribute. However, not all products have user interfaces or have user interfaces that are seldom invoked or invoked only once during installation and configuration of the product. For such products, a usability study may have little value.

3.4.2 Checklists

Checklists are an effective means by which to determine whether or not a product possesses very specific nonmeasurable attributes or attribute elements. From the example cited above, COSQA Software's customers want "a quick-start or getting-started manual" as part of the product. By placing this attribute element on a final QA checklist, you will be certain to check for its existence prior to releasing the product.

3.5   METRICS DEFINITION PROCESS

As stated earlier, metrics allow us to answer two of the most important product development questions: During the development process, *will we* produce a product that meets or exceeds customer requirements, and at the end of the development process, *have we* produced a product that meets or exceeds their requirements? In part, these questions are answered through the use of metrics. To answer them accurately, the right set of metrics must be selected or developed. For example, if you are developing a product that will never change, should you select or develop a metric that allows you to determine whether or not the product is extensible?

In this section, we will develop a set of metrics that will allow us to answer the two most important product development questions for the fictitious customers of COSQA Software. The process is really quite simple, but, as with any process, you should always look for ways to tailor it to suit the specific needs of your environment. Too often, in our industry and others, we look for off the shelf solutions to problems that are not off the shelf. Each environment presents unique challenges, demands, and requirements. Applying or developing any process in an organization requires careful consideration and accommodation of the organizational context. As we build the metrics set for our example, I will point out places where organizational context should be considered before settling on a particular metric.

3.5.1 Process Defined

The metrics definition process follows a logical progression from a quality attributes set to a metrics set. The process begins by explicitly identifying individual attribute elements in each quality attribute. Then, each element is examined and the question is asked: "Can this attribute element be measured?" If the answer is yes, then the question that follows is: "Is there a predefined measurement that can be used?" If the answer is yes, then the question that follows is: "Is there an acceptable value or values to associate with the measurement?" If such a value or values exist, they are associated with the measurement and become a metric. If such a value or values do not exist they must then be defined; otherwise a metric cannot be defined. Finally, the question is asked: "Is there another predefined measurement that can be used?" If that answer is yes, the loop is repeated until no additional predefined measurements exist that satisfy the process. It is better represented as a flow diagram (Figure 3-1).

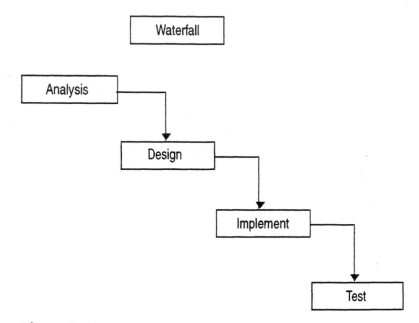

Figure 3–1

Following the diagram along its various paths reveals the simplicity of the metrics definition process. But, as with most other processes, application of the process to solve a specific problem often proves to be much more difficult. The simplest scenario is where all attributes and attribute elements can be measured and predefined measurements exist. The most complex scenario is where none of the attributes and attribute elements can be measured. For most quality attributes sets, the majority of the elements can be measured using predefined measurements. In the next section, we will apply this process to derive a metrics set from the quality attributes set of the customers of COSQA Software.

3.5.2 Process Applied

This section will examine the process in detail by developing metrics for several of the quality attributes found in the example quality attributes set. Following the process defined above, the creation of the metrics set begins by explicitly identifying the individual elements of the first quality attribute from the quality attributes set.

Ease of Use

1. COSQA Software's customers prefer to purchase software products that don't require them to read the manual or use the on-line help facilities. They look for products with Graphical User Interfaces (GUIs) that "look and feel" like other products that they use regularly, such as their word processors and spreadsheet programs. Those programs have what they call "intuitive" user interfaces, which is another way of saying that they can learn the product by playing

with it for a short period of time without consulting the manual.

2. They also prefer products that have a GUI that is sparsely populated with buttons and pop-up (or pull-down) menus, leaving a large work area in which they can create their frequent masterpieces.

Notice that this quality attribute has been divided into its individual elements. This was done to show that there is not always a one-to-one relationship between sentences and attribute elements. For example, the first attribute element consists of three sentences. And, the second attribute element consists of a single sentence.

Can the first attribute element be directly measured? The answer is no! To determine whether or not the product possesses this attribute, a metrics alternative must be defined. In this case, a suitable alternative might be to conduct a usability study where participants who regularly use the word processor and spreadsheet programs mentioned in the attribute are asked to solve a problem using the product without consulting the user manual or on-line help facility. Following the completion of the exercise, they should be asked questions such as, "Does the product look and feel like the word processor and spreadsheet applications that they use?" and "Was the user interface intuitive or did they find themselves tempted to consult the documentation to determine how the product works?"

Can the second attribute element be measured? The answer is yes! Is there a predefined measurement? None of the measurements found in the metrics bucket count GUI items; therefore the answer is no! Consequently, we must define a new metric. The attribute element clearly states that customers desire "... a GUI that is sparsely populated with buttons and pop-up (or pull-down menus)...". A simple count of such GUI elements will allow us to determine whether or not the product possesses this quality attribute. For this measurement to become a metric, an acceptable value must be selected. What do you do when the quality attribute does not explicitly specify an acceptable value or values? Look at the other attribute elements and possibly the other attributes. In our example, the preceding attribute element states, "They look for products with Graphical User Interfaces (GUIs) that 'look and feel' like other products that they use regularly, such as their word processors and spreadsheet programs." By examining the various GUIs of other products that the customers use, a suitable acceptable value can be set. In some cases, though, your search for an acceptable value or values will end in vain. Guessing may be your only recourse. In such situations, your guess should be tested for accuracy during the beta phase of your test cycle.

Now, the process is repeated for the third quality attribute. Notice that there is only one attribute element despite the fact that several sentences describe the attribute.

Defect Tolerance

1. To COSQA Software's customers, defects such as some typos in message strings and in help text as well as minor disparities between documented and actual behavior or function will be tolerated until the next release. On the other hand, they will not toler-

ate defects that alter or destroy their works in progress or that adversely affect their productivity. Such defects will likely drive them to abandon the product in favor of a product that may be less robust but more reliable. They consider defects such as general exceptions, hangs, data corruption, and long delays between operations to be intolerable defects.

Can this attribute be directly measured? The answer is yes! Is there a predefined measurement? Again, the answer is yes! A metric from the metrics bucket above, *defects by severity*, can be used to determine whether or not the product possesses this particular quality attribute. To become a metric, however, we must define the various severity levels and acceptable values for those levels.

The attribute suggests two levels of severity. We will designate severity 1 defects as general exceptions, hangs, data corruption, and long delays between operations, and severity 2 defects as typos in message strings and in help text and minor disparities between documented and actual behavior or function. Given the measurement, what are the acceptable values for each? The quality attribute states that customers will tolerate some severity 2 defects and no severity 1 defects. Since the attribute does not explicitly specify the number of severity 2 defects that the customer will tolerate, we will choose 12 as an acceptable value. For severity 1 defects, the acceptable value is 0. We now have a metric to use to determine whether or not the product possesses this particular quality attribute.

Finally, the process will be repeated for one more quality attribute, attribute number 5 from the quality attributes set.

Defect Impact

1. COSQA Software's customers see themselves as highly productive people who prefer to work on several things at once. They often start several applications on their workstations simultaneously, jumping from one to another. Many of COSQA Software's customers have had an experience where they noticed that whenever they jumped from their word processor to a particular vendor's desktop publishing system, they had to wait several minutes for the view to redraw. The desktop publishing system developers decided to optimize memory usage, sacrificing view redrawing performance. They assumed that most users would not switch from application to application while using their product; consequently view redrawing would be infrequent. To save memory, they decided to save the current view on disk, retrieving it whenever they needed to perform a redraw. This design decision saved a large amount of memory but sacrificed redrawing performance. Though some users might appreciate the designers' effort to decrease memory usage, COSQA Software's customers viewed the resulting poor performance of view redrawing as a major defect since it severely impacted their productivity.

Can this attribute be directly measured? The answer is yes, however, such a defect would be classified as a severity 1 defect and since no severity 1 defects are allowed, is it necessary to define a metric? In this case, the answer is no since the metric defined for another quality attribute effectively eliminates the need to define one for this quality attribute.

3.6 CONCLUSION

The two goals for this chapter were to develop an understanding of and appreciation for metrics and other methods of analysis and to define a process that can be followed to build a set of specific metrics from a quality attributes set. To achieve the first goal, the term "metric" was defined; a metrics classification was defined, product- versus process-oriented metrics, and several other well-known metrics were presented from each class. To achieve the second goal, a metrics definition process was defined and applied to COSQA Software's customers' quality attributes set to define a metrics set. During the application of the process, we discovered that not all quality attributes are directly measurable. In such cases, alternatives such as usability studies and checklists must be used to determine whether or not the product possesses those quality attributes.

Now that we thoroughly understand the customer quality requirements, how do we actually perform the measurements? For example, in the opening analogy, the physician often uses a metric known as body temperature to help him determine whether or not his patient is healthy. Body temperature can be measured in several ways. The most popular method is to use a thermometer. For software, testing is used to perform the measurements. Various test methods exist and they will be reviewed in the next chapter.

Chapter 4

Test Methods, Types, and Tools

4.1 INTRODUCTION

Customer-oriented software quality assurance defines a process that first captures customer requirements, representing them as quality attributes, and then translates those requirements into metrics. Testing is the means by which you determine whether or not a product meets or exceeds the baseline of acceptability established by the metrics. Using the patient-physician analogy, tests are the thermometers and sphygmomanometers of the quality assurance and test engineer.

Tests can be classified by method and type. Most readers should be familiar with such terms as stress tests, system tests, unit tests, whitebox testing, blackbox testing, and so forth. Whitebox and blackbox testing are examples of test methods and stress tests, system tests, and unit tests are examples of test types. Selecting the right methods, the right test types, and then the right tests is perhaps the most challenging aspect of the customer-oriented quality assurance process. Quite often, tests are chosen arbitrarily. For example, stress tests, often designed to push a system beyond its design limits for some period of time, are often used to determine whether or not a product is ready for release. What if the product is never used in an environment that pushes it beyond its design limits? Is it necessary that such tests be used to determine whether or not the product is ready for release? No! They might be used for other purposes, but not to determine readiness for release.

Once an appropriate method or methods and type or types have been chosen, tests must be developed. Many choices exist here as well. For example, you may be able to purchase a commercial test suite to test your product. If you are developing a C compiler, there are several well-known C compiler test suites on the market including the Plum Hall and C-torture test suites. You may need to develop your own tests from scratch. You may also be able to purchase a test tool that simplifies the test development process. As you will see, the choice you make depends upon the results of the previous step in the customer-oriented software quality assurance process.

There are two goals for this chapter: to review various test methods and test types and to learn how to select the ones needed to develop a test suite that will determine whether or not the product satisfies or exceeds customer quality requirements as represented by the metrics set. Once the methods are selected, test cases are developed. The set of all test cases developed is referred to as the test suite. If developed properly, the test suite, on execution, will give you the data you need to determine whether or not the product is ready for release.

4.2 TEST METHODS

A method is simply a procedure one follows to achieve some end. For example, a structured programming method known as stepwise refinement is a procedure one follows to design and implement a program by beginning with a problem whose abstract solution is iteratively refined until it is reduced to its smallest constituent components. A test method is simply a procedure one follows to create a set of tests, or test suite, that can be used to determine whether or not a product satisfies some set of quality related criteria. For customer-oriented software quality assurance, the quality-related criteria include meeting or exceeding customer quality requirements as defined by their quality attributes set. The test method or methods chosen, therefore, must support the attainment of that end.

Two popular test methods are reviewed in this section: blackbox and whitebox. I have read about and participated in many debates concerning the use of these two methods. Many believe that only one test method or the other should be applied. My position is that the method or methods chosen should provide a means to an end. Achieving that end may require the application of more than one method. In those cases, combining methods becomes necessary. Strict conformance to one method or another will limit one's ability to achieve the desired result.

4.2.1 Blackbox

There are two ways to look at a system: from the outside looking in and from the inside looking out. The blackbox test method is applied from the former vantage point. The term "blackbox" simply means to view the system as if it were a sealed box whose particular internal contents are unimportant. Of importance, however, are the end-user visible interfaces, features, and behaviors of the box.

For example, a word processor when viewed as a blackbox has an end-user visible interface, and many different features and behaviors. The user interface presents various menu items, tool bars, status information, and the document being edited. When a menu item such as "Save" is selected, a behavior can be observed. In this case, the behavior is that the file is written to permanent storage for later retrieval. When toolbar buttons are depressed, other behaviors can be observed, such as printing the document, aligning a highlighted block of text, or changing the font of a highlighted block of text.

When the blackbox test method is applied to test the word processor in the example above, tests are developed that ensure that the end-user visible interface, features, and behaviors are observed. For example, since the "Save" button writes the document to permanent storage for later retrieval, a blackbox test case should be developed that ensures that the file can be retrieved after a "Save" operation has been performed. The save operation may also prompt the user to confirm whether or not the current version of the permanent file should be overwritten. In this case, another blackbox test case should be developed that ensures that the overwrite feature exhibits the desired behavior.

The blackbox test method ignores the details of what is inside the box. Intuitively, this makes sense since the user has no interest in what is inside; rather, they are interested in whether or not the product works correctly. But, sometimes, a knowledge of the contents of the box is necessary. Developing tests based on such a knowledge is the subject of the next section of this chapter.

4.2.2 Whitebox

The whitebox test method is applied from the vantage point of the inside of the box looking out. The term "whitebox" simply means to view the system as if it were an open box whose contents are very important. To develop tests from this perspective you must have the appropriate knowledge and skills to interpret design specifications and code.

Whitebox tests are designed to exploit weaknesses in a product's design and implementation. For example, suppose that upon examination of a product's design specification, a test engineer discovers that the application caches data in an in-memory cache until the user saves the file. Suppose that either the system or the application crashes before the save operation is performed. Is data lost? A whitebox test could be developed that modifies a file and then intentionally causes the system to reboot before a save operation is performed. In contrast, since the blackbox test method is applied without an awareness of the product's design and implementation, the test developer will likely fail to develop such test cases.

4.3   TYPES OF TESTS

Test cases are typically classified as one of the following: unit, component, integration, system, scenario, or stress. Unit tests represent the least complex of the tests. Problems discovered by unit tests are typically the easiest problems to correct. Component tests tend to be more complex than unit tests and problems discovered by them are usually more difficult to correct. Each subsequent classification corresponds to an increasingly complicated set of test cases that tend to find problems that require lengthier analysis and defect fix times. The following subsections discuss each classification in more detail.

4.3.1   Unit

The purpose of a unit test is to test the individual functions that together provide a single application primitive. For example, from a blackbox perspective, the word processor's save operation is an application primitive. When the save operation is selected, most word processors prompt the user for additional information such as the directory in which the file should be saved, the file's name, and access control information. To test this primitive thoroughly, a set of unit tests are developed that test the middle and end or boundary cases of this primitive using every combination of the primitive's options followed by testing all error conditions and then exception conditions.

A "middle" test case is one that uses a value that falls in the middle of a range of possible valid values while "end" or "boundary" cases use values that lie at either extremes of that range. A test for an error condition intentionally performs an illegal operation to determine whether or not the application handles the error appropriately. Finally, an exception test is a test that seeks to cause the application to fail in some non-deterministic way. For the case of the word processor's save primitive, unit tests might be developed to test whether or not all combinations of middle values work correctly, followed by all combinations of end or boundary values, then error conditions, and finally exception conditions.

4.3.2 Component

The purpose of a component test is to test a set of logically related units. For example, from a whitebox perspective, let's say that the save operation in the previous example consists of ten different C language functions. Each function represents a unit, while all ten represent a component since they are logically related to each other. In this case, a set of unit tests are developed to test each function while additional tests or component tests are developed to test all the functions working together to achieve some larger end—saving a file to permanent storage. Like unit tests, component tests are developed that test the middle and end or boundary cases followed by testing error conditions and then exception conditions.

4.3.3 System

The purpose of a system test is to test a set of logically related components. For example, the save operation referred to in previous examples is a system component that is logically related to the component that provides document editing and to the component that provides page layout. When a document is saved, the modified content of the document as well as the page layout are saved to permanent storage. Working in concert, these three components provide a capability that each alone does not provide. Testing this synergism among components is the goal of a system test. Like its predecessors, system tests are developed that test the middle and end or boundary cases followed by testing error conditions and then exception conditions.

4.3.4 Scenario

The purpose of a scenario test is to model customer configurations and usage. For example, suppose that your product, a word processing application, is used by your customers in two different ways. First, they use the application to create reports that are, on average, less than five pages in length. Further, the documents are always E-mailed as attachments using a variety of E-mail applications that support attached documents. Occasionally, the documents are printed on low-end black and white printers. Second, they use the application to create multisection books that range in length from between one hundred and two hundred pages with embedded diagrams and color graphics. The books are never E-mailed as attachments; however, they are often printed on color printers. Scenario tests, in this case, would perform operations like those described in the previous example and using the same configurations. In other words, test cases that involve developing thousand-page reports that are printed on high-end black and white printers and that are never E-mailed would not be performed in lieu of test cases that model customer configurations and usage.

4.3.5 Stress

The purpose of a stress test is to push a product to its limits and possibly beyond. Such tests often uncover unexpected design and implementation flaws that would otherwise go undetected. For example, memory leaks, race conditions, dead locks, and other similar and difficult-to-find problems are typically uncovered by such testing.

Like the other tests, however, the value of such testing and the limits to which a product is pushed should depend on customer requirements. What is stressful is relative. Some customers may regularly push an application to its limits while others never approach those limits. Stress testing is also used by many companies to determine the limits to which their product can be pushed. In other words, their design does not explicitly address or cannot predict the product's limitations. Following such testing, the limitations are typically documented and the product shipped (assuming the limitations are satisfactory). Other times, the limitations exposed during such testing reveal a need to redesign some part of the product.

Stress testing is often misused by QA organizations to thwart the release of a product. Any product of even moderate complexity, regardless of how carefully designed and implemented, can be broken by stress testing. What must be determined is whether or not the stress tests create a scenario that your customers are likely to encounter. If such an encounter is likely, then the problems discovered by such tests must be resolved. Otherwise, solving them would be a bonus but not necessary.

4.3.6 Other

A number of other types of tests such as usability tests and performance analysis tests exist. Ultimately, however, the test types chosen for a particular quality assurance effort should be driven by the customer quality attributes set. Section 4.5 gives several examples of this selection process.

4.4 COMMERCIAL TEST TOOLS

As product complexity increases, development and QA cycles shorten, and companies continue to release products at an ever-increasing rate, dependence on tools that simplify and improve the productivity of the quality assurance effort increases.

When I started my career in the early eighties, commercial test tools were not generally available. At Data General, one of the earliest projects assigned to me was to develop a test suite to test the terminal services component of the AOS/VS II operating system. The AOS/VS II operating system was a proprietary operating system designed to operate on Data General's MV platform family. Unlike the UNIX and Microsoft Windows operating systems of today, system calls or calls to kernel services were very difficult to make. Large data structures had to be allocated and initialized. Most system calls required calls to a number of support routines prior to making the desired call. One unit test case would require from between two and four pages of C code (back then a page was about 66 lines of line printer output.) To thoroughly test just one feature of the read system call, for example, line editing, hundreds of test cases or thousands of lines of code had to be written!

To simplify test development, I designed my first test tool. When finished, I was able to develop a significantly larger number of test cases over a much shorter period of time than would have been possible using the old method of test case development. For the case of the read system call, only two command lines were required to direct the tool to perform the desired test operation. Rather than thousands of lines of code, only hundreds of lines of command directives were required to thoroughly test the editing capability of the read system call. In fact, the tool simplified the task of developing terminal services tests so much that the development team adopted it as their official terminal services debugging tool. It's too bad that the tool was designed to test a proprietary operating system! Had I designed such a tool to test UNIX operating system calls, I might be a wealthy man today!

The utility of test tools was quite apparent to me back in those days. Unfortunately, it would be awhile before commercially available tools would become generally available. Until that time arrived, each new test development effort that I embarked upon involved developing a substantial amount of infrastructure code—code that had nothing to do with testing the product. Today, products like QA Partner from Segue, WinRunner from Mercury Interactive, and MS Test from Microsoft provide the test infrastructure allowing the quality assurance or test development engineer to focus on test case development.

In addition to simplifying test development, test tools are available on the market that gather certain metrics such as test coverage, number of lines of code, number of modules, number of function points, number of decision points, and percentage of code executed by test cases. Products such as Veritas from Veritas Corporation and PureCoverage from Rational Software, Inc., are examples of such commercially available tools. These tools are useful to the extent that they allow you to determine whether or not your product satisfies your customers' quality attributes. For example, some companies define a code coverage metric that specifies the percentage of code that must be executed by test cases during the formal test phase of the product development cycle. What percentage of code must be covered to have a quality product? 90 percent? 100 percent? For practitioners of customer-oriented software quality assurance, the answers to such questions are found in the quality attributes set.

4.5   SELECTING THE RIGHT METHODS, TYPES, AND TOOLS

The process of selecting the right test methods, test types, and test tools begins by reexamining the example quality attributes set. For example, recall from Chapter 3 that COSQA Software's customers' quality attributes set contains the following attribute and associated metrics:

Attribute:

Ease of use

> COSQA Software's customers prefer to purchase software products that don't require them to read the manual or use the on-line help facilities. They look for products with Graphical User Interfaces (GUIs) that "look and feel" like other products that they use regularly, such as their word processors and spreadsheet programs. Those programs have what they call "intuitive" user interfaces, which is another way of saying that they can learn the product by playing with it for a short period of time without consulting the manual. They also prefer products that have a GUI that is sparsely populated with buttons and pop-up (or pull-down) menus, leaving a large work area in which they can create their masterpieces.

Metrics:

<None defined>

Which methods, types, and tools are appropriate to determine whether or not the product satisfies the quality requirements expressed by this attribute? It's unlikely that an automated test tool will be useful. More appropriate, however, is a usability study. In such a study, end users, typically existing customers, are invited to participate in a product usability study. The session begins with a product tutorial. Next, the participants are given a series of tasks to perform and then asked to comment on their experience performing each task. The results are compiled and analyzed. Finally, changes are made to the product to address deficiencies.

As another example, consider the following quality attribute from COSQA Software's customers' quality attributes set.

Attribute:

Ease of use

COSQA Software's customers expect all documentation to be on-line and context sensitive. They also prefer comprehensive and voluminous documentation. They noted that a quick-start or getting-started manual is indispensable. They cannot stand searching through documentation to figure out something as simple as installing the product, invoking it, and using its most elementary features. Also, they find errors in documentation inexcusable. They believe that any product with poorly edited documentation must contain coding errors that will someday surface at a most inopportune moment, destroying one of their works in progress. Fearing such a disaster, they may not purchase a product known to have poorly edited documentation.

Metrics:

Documentation Error Count = 0

Again, which methods, types, and tools are appropriate to determine whether or not the product satisfies the quality requirements expressed by this attribute? For this case, several methods can be used. Manual test procedures can be used to determine if the documentation is on-line, context sensitive, and includes a quick-start manual. A documentation editor can be assigned the task of determining whether or not the documentation is comprehensive and voluminous. A usability study can be conducted to assess the usefulness of the quick start manual. Finally, test engineers can be assigned the task of reviewing the documentation for accuracy.

As a final example, consider the following quality attribute.

Attribute:

Ease of use

To COSQA Software's customers, defects such as some typos in message strings and in help text as well as minor disparities between documented and actual behavior or function will be tolerated until the next release. On the other hand, they will not tolerate defects that alter or destroy their works in progress or that adversely affect their productivity. Such defects will likely drive them to abandon the product in favor of a product that may be less robust but more reliable. They consider defects such as general exceptions, hangs, data corruption, and long delays between operations to be intolerable defects.

Metrics:

Defects by Severity (Severity 1 = 0, Severity 2 = 12)

This attribute calls for a comprehensive test suite that consists of unit, system, scenario, and stress tests. Particular attention should be paid to the scenario and stress tests. Test scenarios should be defined that simulate the most complex of the customer environments. Stress tests should be defined that push the system to its design limits to determine whether or not general exceptions, hangs, and data corruption results. Finally, performance data should be collected during scenario testing to determine whether or not long delays occur between operations. Since the number of tests and the complexity of the test environment are likely to be very high in this case, a test tool or tools may be of great assistance.

4.6   CONCLUSION

The two goals for this chapter were to review various test methods and test types and to learn how to select the ones needed to develop a test suite that will determine whether or not the product satisfies or exceeds customer quality requirements as represented by the metrics set. As can be seen in the example, the process of selecting the right test methods and test types is not particularly formal. That is, you must look at each attribute along with its associated metric, if it has one, then look at the test methods and types at your disposal, and finally, through a leap of judgment, and sometimes faith, select the right methods and types to achieve the end. The "leap of judgment" part is what makes this part of the process informal and, perhaps, the most difficult to apply.

Chapter 5

The QA Program

5.1 INTRODUCTION

The first four chapters of this book focus on creating the
right test suite for your product. Creating the right test
suite is just one item on a much longer list of activities
that an organization should engage in to successfully
create a product that satisfies its customer quality
requirements. This longer list of activities includes
things such as defining and following a product development process that may include project planning and
project management activities, using configuration
management systems, and using a defect tracking tool

to keep track of problems from the point in time that they are discovered through, hopefully, their resolution.

The goal of this chapter is to examine various activities that you and your organization can engage in and tools you can use to assist you with the production of a product that satisfies customer quality requirements. You may choose to expand the set discussed here for many reasons. For example, your organization may be attempting to move to a higher level of capability as defined by the SEI Capability Maturity Model or your organization may be in the process of registering to ISO 9000 (both are discussed in the next chapter). In either case, my recommendation is that your organization should at least engage in the activities discussed in this chapter.

5.2   PROCESSES

5.2.1   What Is a Process?

Put simply, a process is a series of steps followed to achieve some end. Everyone, everyday, follows a number of processes. You follow a process when you wake up in the morning, for example, you get out of bed, drink a cup of coffee, iron your clothes, and take a shower, or when you drive your car, or follow a physical fitness regimen, or when you engage in a time management planning exercise, and so on.

To clarify, let's say that someone, let's call him Traveler, wants to drive his car to the grocery store. What's the first thing that he should do after sitting down behind the wheel of his car? Put on his seat belt, perhaps? Adjust the mirrors? Turn the car on? Regardless of which step he executes first, at some point he must turn the car on, then engage the transmission, and proceed to the market. The process followed will ultimately lead him to his goal; the grocery store. Notice that this process can be described at various levels of detail. For example, let's say that another person, let's call her Passer-by, asks Traveler how to get to the grocery store. Traveler could begin by saying, "First, retrieve the keys for your automobile. Then, open the door. Next, sit in the car and insert the key in the ignition." At this point, Passer-by may grow impatient and tell Traveler that she already knows how to drive her car; she simply wants to know what roads to follow to reach the grocery store. Traveler then, after apologizing profusely for insulting Passer-by's intelligence, proceeds to describe the series of roads, distances, and turns that must be followed to reach the grocery store. Finally, Passer-by, realizing that the process is considerably more complex than she anticipated, asks Traveler to write it down. While writing, Traveler realizes that many people ask him how to reach the grocery store. He decides to make copies to hand out to others that ask in the future.

With directions to the grocery store in hand, Passer-by departs. Now, let's say that en route, she encounters a serious accident that completely blocks the way. Should she turn around and go home? Or, should she seek an alternate route that will allow her to traverse the obstruction and proceed to the grocery store? Most likely, she will seek an alternate route. In other words, there is both a "normal" process for getting to the grocery store and an "exception" process to deal with unexpected obstacles. In this case, the exception process is the alternate route that she will follow to reach the gro-

cery store. However, many other things can wrong on
the way to the grocery store. Her car may break down.
She might get into an accident or be victimized by
crime. Should she anticipate every possible failure scenario and extend her process to respond to each one?
Perhaps, however, she should be prepared to starve as
she spends countless hours, days, or even weeks defining ways to handle events that are very unlikely to
occur. Finally, it may not be possible to anticipate
everything that might go wrong. And, even it were possible, it might not be possible to develop an alternate
path to the goal.

After traversing the obstacle, Passer-by encounters
an undocumented fork in the road. Beside the fork, she
notices a sign that indicates that the city of Byte is to
the right and the city of Bit is to the left. She remem-
bers an advertisement from last Sunday's newspaper
that mentioned that the grocery store is in the city of
Byte. Though Traveler did not specify a process for
Passer-by to follow should she encounter an undocumented fork in the road, she was able to proceed down
the correct path. Upon reaching the grocery store,
Passer-by realizes that she has been to that grocery
store before and that there is a much more efficient
path. She calls Traveler and tells him of the undocumented fork in the road and about the more efficient
path. Traveler acknowledges the improvement by
updating the recorded process.

A process, then, is simply a series of steps that
when followed lead to some end. A process almost
always defines the "normal" case and may define ways
to handle "exceptions." If sufficiently complex or if more
than one person must follow the process, it might be

documented. Finally, it may include a feedback mechanism that allows for adjustments.

All software development organizations, whether consisting of one engineer or thousands, follow a process. You may be saying to yourself, "What's that you say? All software organizations follow a process? Surely, you haven't worked for my company!" Although your organization may best be characterized as anarchical, if you look closely enough, you will see that a process is being followed. Chances are, the software development process that your organization follows can be described as a linear progression from concept or idea followed by the development of a design to code writing, then to testing and finally to release. Such a process is referred to as a waterfall process. Other kinds of processes exist and they will be discussed in the following sections. Is one process better than another? Each process has strengths and weaknesses. The best process is the one that allows you to achieve the results you desire. For practitioners of customer-oriented software quality assurance, the desired result is to produce a product that meets or exceeds customer quality requirements as expressed through their quality attributes set.

5.2.2 Types of Processes

5.2.2.1 Introduction

A process defines a sequence of steps to perform in order to achieve some end. There are many different types of processes followed within the software industry. For example, most software development organizations follow what is called the waterfall process. Other popular processes include prototyping and the iterative process. There are a number of others; however, these are the most common and they are discussed in detail next.

5.2.2.2   Waterfall

The waterfall process consists of a number of phases where the activities performed during each phase are logically related and unique with respect to the activities performed in other phases. Each phase is distinct; in other words, it has an identifiable start and end (see Figure 5–1). Strictly followed, once a phase has been completed, it is never repeated. During the first phase, or analysis phase, the product requirements, development plan, and the test, QA, documentation, and manufacturing plans are developed. During the second phase, the product is designed. The primary activity in the third phase is implementation of the design. And, finally, the implementation is tested in the fourth phase.

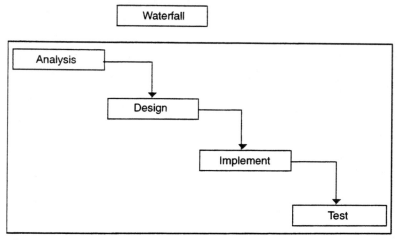

Figure 5–1

5.2.2.3   Prototyping

The prototyping process is the waterfall process preceded by a phase where a working model of the system is developed. A working model is a model that, to the user, looks and operates like the "real thing." However, internally, the prototype may be incomplete or in some non-final form. The prototype is developed to validate the requirements and to test design options before proceeding with the development of the final requirements, design, and implementation (see Figure 5–2). Some followers of this process believe that the prototype must be disposed of following its completion. Others, like myself, believe that at least parts of the prototype can be reused in the final product.

This process attempts to overcome the primary weakness of the waterfall process: That the requirements for the system must be completely defined before moving on to the next phase in the development cycle. Development of a prototype gives an organization a means to refine and, hopefully, completely specify the requirements for the system. Once the requirements are completely specified, development of the "real thing" can proceed by following the traditional waterfall process.

5.2.2.4   Iterative

Unfortunately, more often than not, development of the prototype does not provide enough information to develop a complete specification of the requirements. Consequently, the prototype process breaks down during later phases when the requirements must be changed. The iterative process evolved from this weak-

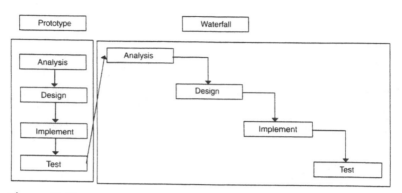

Figure 5–2

ness in the prototyping process. Like the prototyping process, the iterative process produces a working version of the product during the first phase. Unlike the prototyping process, the end result of the first phase is not automatically discarded. Also, unlike the prototyping process, the end result of the first phase is an incomplete, but working subset of the final product. Both internally and externally, the product is in near final form. On the other hand, in the prototyping process the end result of the first phase may appear to the user to be complete but internally may be far from final form.

For the iterative process, each phase following the first is an incremental refinement of its predecessor and there is no fixed limit to the number of iterations that can be performed (see Figure 5–3). However, too few iterations may degrade the process to either the prototyping or waterfall process. Too many iterations may add unnecessary overhead to the project.

For both the waterfall and prototyping processes to succeed, requirements must be completely specified

early in the project. In other words, after the requirements are specified, they must not be changed once the
phase during which they are developed has ended. Anyone who has ever developed a complex software application or system will tell you that their requirements are
rarely if ever completely specified for a number of reasons. Some of the more common reasons are that over
time the problem being solved changes, unique user
requirements are not anticipated before the product is
deployed, the needs and wants of users change, and the
technology used to solve the problem changes at a rate
that quickly makes a solution obsolete.

The advantage of the iterative process over the other
two covered in this book is that it is designed to accommodate change, that is, change in product requirements,
change in design, change in implementation, and change
in test. It accomplishes this by treating the entire software development process as a series of mini-waterfalls
that begins with the development of a subset of the system and from mini-waterfall to mini-waterfall
progresses toward what becomes an implementation of
the system that satisfies the requirements. The other
advantage it has over the other two discussed is that at
the end of each phase, or mini-waterfall, a working, fully
tested, subset of the product is available. If, as we will
see later, it becomes necessary to release the product
before the entire system is implemented, this process
can accommodate such a need. The others cannot since
an intermediate, fully tested implementation is not
available until the very end of the project.

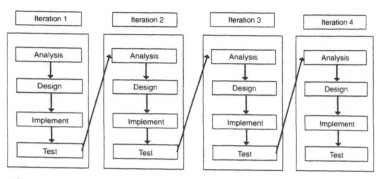

Figure 5–3

5.3   SELECTING THE RIGHT PROCESS TO FOLLOW

5.3.1   Introduction

Popular use of the waterfall process for software development can be traced back to the late 1960s. Back then, both computers and their software were most often designed to solve very specific problems from the venues of mathematics and science. Also, during that period, computing time was very expensive, computing resources were very limited, and software development tools were either nonexistent or very primitive. The things that we take for granted today, such as third+-generation languages, source-level debuggers, sophisticated GUIs, and the like, either did not exist or were used very infrequently. Software developers had to analyze the requirements very carefully, design a solution, and write and test the code by hand to avoid incurring unnecessary computer charges and delays associated with limited resource availability. As the set of problems solved by software systems expanded from narrow in scope in the early days to include broad in scope today, it became increasingly more difficult to completely specify the requirements for those systems. Consequently, the prototyping process became a popular software development process to follow since it provides a means to validate the requirements, ultimately enabling the development of a more complete requirements specification.

Quite often, though, the prototyping process suffers from the same weakness that the waterfall process suffers from: The requirements for the system cannot be completely specified. Rather than abandon the project or get stuck in the requirements phase and never delivering a product, the iterative process supports the development of a product where the requirements, design, implementation, and testing undergo a series of refinements that over time lead to a complete specification of the requirements and a product that completely satisfies those requirements.

Selecting the right process for a product development effort to follow is relatively straightforward. The first step is to identify the scope of the problem. The second step is to factor in the importance of releasing the product at a particular point in time. The third step is to determine whether or not the tools available for the project will support or compromise the success of the project when following a particular process.

5.3.2 Scope of Problem

The waterfall process works well for cases where the problem to be solved is narrow in scope. Cases that are broad in scope, however, tend to be very difficult, if not impossible, to specify completely. Without a complete specification of requirements, the waterfall process quickly breaks down. If the development of a complete requirements specification proves to be impossible, the waterfall process would be a poor choice to follow.

The prototype process model works well for cases where the problem to be solved is broader in scope. Unfortunately, there is no simple way to determine whether or not the scope of the problem being solved is too large for the prototyping process to be effective. To determine whether or not the scope is too broad for the prototyping process, you must have a high degree of confidence that the development of a complete specification will be possible following the development of the prototype. If that feeling of confidence is present, chances are that the scope of the problem is not too broad. If, however you feel a low degree of confidence that it will be possible to develop a complete specification following the development of the prototype, the scope of the problem is probably too broad.

Finally, the iterative process works well for cases where the problem to be solved is broad in scope and where the development of a complete requirements specification is not possible. This process is specifically designed for such cases. By treating the development process as a series of mini-waterfalls that are repeatedly refined, the end result is the development of an application or system that solves the problem as specified by the requirements.

5.3.3 Schedule

Another factor that must be considered when selecting a process is project schedule. For the waterfall process, the project schedule is usually set during the first phase. For the prototyping process, the project schedule is usually set following the development of the prototype. And, for the iterative process, the project schedule is usually set early but revised repeatedly along with the other project deliverables. Regardless of which process is followed, it is often the case that the date selected is arbitrary. Other times, the date selected lies within what is called a market window of opportunity. The market window of opportunity for a product is the period of time during which demand for the product is predicted to be at its highest. Hitting the window at the right moment is crucial to acquiring the greatest share of the market. Accurate project schedules, therefore, are very important. Unfortunately, both the waterfall and prototyping process have poor track records for predicting when a project will finish.

Why do these two processes consistently fail to predict project schedule accurately? The main reason is that if during a downstream phase a problem is encountered that was introduced in an upstream phase, the only recourse is to return to the upstream phase, resolve the problem, and revisit the phases that follow. When upstream activities are revisited, the changes ripple all the way down to the bottom, ultimately pushing the schedule out. For example, a performance problem discovered during the test phase usually requires a change to the design. Once the design is changed, the code must be changed, and the testing repeated. But, since the problem wasn't uncovered until very late in the cycle, the schedule slip is at the end of the project, often pushing the delivery out beyond the window of opportunity. In other words, changes to schedule required as a result of having to revisit earlier phases can have a large impact on the overall schedule.

The iterative process isn't necessarily any better at predicting when a project will finish; however, since the schedule goes through a series of refinements like the other project deliverables, the schedule becomes more accurate over time. And, since revisiting an earlier phase is done within the context of a mini-waterfall, the ripple effect is contained and usually has a much smaller effect on the schedule. Also, at the end of each iteration, a working subset of the system is produced. If the schedule is slipping past the window of opportunity, the company has the option to release a subset of the product with the rest to follow in a subsequent release. With the other processes, no such option exists.

When choosing a process to follow, the importance of delivering the product at a particular point in time must be considered. Let's consider some of the combinations. If the problem to be solved is narrow in scope and the window of opportunity is wide, then the waterfall process will suffice. However, if the scope of the problem to solve is broad in scope and the window of opportunity is narrow, your chances of success may increase if you follow the prototyping process. If the scope of the problem to solve is wide and the window of opportunity is also wide, then either the prototyping or the iterative processes may work best. Finally, if the scope is wide and the window of opportunity is narrow, you'll then stand a much greater chance of success if you follow the iterative process.

5.3.4   Availability of Tools

The waterfall process was developed during a time when tools in general were relatively unsophisticated.

In particular, compiler technology was very primitive. Most code was written in assembler. Debuggers were very simple and required an in-depth knowledge of the underlying hardware architecture. In those days, debugging was such a painful prospect that code was usually committed to the machine only after being meticulously and painstakingly executed by hand. In fact, for the most part, the code was debugged before ever executing on the system for which it was written. The waterfall process is a good match for product development efforts that are constrained to use primitive development tools.

As tools became more sophisticated, in particular, as assembler gave way to third generation languages like C and source-level debuggers were introduced, less care was necessary during the implementation phase of a product development effort. The pace of software development began to accelerate. It became economical to develop and execute code earlier in the implementation phase since any problems introduced as a result of hastiness could be isolated and removed using a modern debugger. In fact, the economics of code writing was such that working models of the product could be developed to guide the development of the final product or "real thing." It was during this period that the prototyping process became popular.

Since then, compiler and debugger technology has advanced to the point that lay people, using this technology, can develop very sophisticated applications very quickly with very little training. The cost per line of code, both in terms of dollars and time, has reached such a low point that the development of numerous prototypes during a product development effort has become economical. The iterative process is possible because of the existence of such tools and is just now beginning to gain acceptance as a mainstream software development process.

Most new software development is developed using the very latest technologies available. Modern compilers and debuggers make following a process like the iterative process possible. However, there are certainly many new products being developed on legacy systems for which modern compiler and debugger technology are not available. For such projects, it may not be possible or economically practical to follow the iterative process.

5.4 CONFIGURATION MANAGEMENT

5.4.1 Introduction

A configuration is a particular instance of a product. For example, Microsoft Word 7.0 for Windows 95, the product that I'm using to develop this book, is a particular instance of the Microsoft Word product. Other instances (or configurations) of the product include earlier versions, such as version 1.0, 2.0, and the versions that run under the Apple MacIntosh operating system.

Configuration Management (CM) refers to the set of processes and procedures that an organization follows and the tools that it uses to manage the source code from which various configurations of a product are derived. Management of the source code includes specifying and enforcing such policies as restricting access to certain individuals, preventing more than one person from modifying the same code at the same time, restricting the type of code checked in to a particular class, that is, defect repairs versus enhancements, and so forth. Management of the source code also includes defining the content of a particular configuration of the product. Once the content is defined, the specific derivative of the product can be produced. Production refers to the activities engaged in and the tools used to construct the product.

Despite what CM tool vendors tell you, CM can be practiced without sophisticated and often very expensive tools. However, the larger an organization, the bigger the product, and the greater the number of versions of the product, the harder it is to practice CM without the aid of such tools. Now, for a closer look at the three essential components of CM: source code control, production, and problem/defect tracking.

5.4.2 Source Code Control

Source code control refers to the act of controlling access to and changes made to a product's source files. Some CM systems provide mechanisms to enforce access policies. For example, a valid defect number from the defect tracking system must be entered before check-out/check-in is permitted, or approval from a higher authority such as a manager or engineering change committee must be granted before check-out/ check-in is permitted.

Once access to a file is granted, changes to that file can be managed using one of two methods: (1) sequential, and (2) copy-merge. For the sequential method, only one person at a time is permitted to modify the file. This restriction is usually enforced by employing a lock mechanism. In other words, when a module or file is checked out of the source code control system, a lock is engaged, preventing anyone else from checking out the same module or file. Once the lock holder checks the file back in to the source code control system, the lock is disengaged, allowing someone else to check the file out. The positive aspect of the sequential method is that it prevents one person from undoing the work of another. One of its limitations, however, is that anyone else who may need to modify the same file will be blocked until the file is checked in.

For the copy-merge method, many people can independently check out and modify the same modules or files. As each file is checked in, however, it must be merged to prevent one person from overwriting changes made by others. For example, imagine that you and I checked out a file containing the following C function:

```
int sum(int x, int y)
{
    int z;
    z=x+y;
    return z;
}
```

I decide to change the code to return a 0 if the sum of x and y exceeds 10. My copy of the code now looks like

```
int sum(int x, int y)
{
    int z;
    z=x+y;
    if (z > 10)
        z=0;
    return z;
}
```

At the same time, you add a line of code to your copy of the original file that will display the sum before returning. Your copy of the code now looks like

```
int sum(int x, int y)
{
    int z;
    z=x+y;
    printf("%d\n", z);
    return z;
}
```

If I check in my code first, it will take the place of the original. When you check in your code, rather than take the place of my version, it must be merged. In other words, the changes that we made in our copies of the original must be reconciled. Source control systems that support the copy-merge paradigm have tools that automatically merge code in such situations. For this case the merged code would look like

```
int sum(int x, int y)
{
    int z;
    z=x+y;
    if (z > 10)
        z=0;
    printf("%d\n", z);
    return z;
}
```

Automatic merging, however, is not foolproof. You should always review the results of a merge to make sure that the tools did not create an abomination. Also, there are times when the tools cannot reconcile the differences between two variants of the original. In such situations, the utilities somehow flag the conflict. Hand merging becomes necessary.

The positive aspect of the copy-merge method is that engineers are never blocked. On the other hand, merging is not foolproof and must be reviewed carefully. The time needed to conduct such reviews may negate the benefit of not blocking!

Putting aside customer-oriented software quality assurance for a moment, source code control is almost always a necessity for projects that have more than one team member. With respect to customer-oriented quality assurance, source code control may be necessary in order to use a metric such as "Number of source code changes over time must decrease by 10 percent per week."

5.4.3 Production

5.4.3.1   Introduction

Production can be divided into two categories: version management and construction. Version management refers to the set of policies and procedures that, when enforced, define the specific content of a particular version of the product, that is, the set of sources needed to construct a particular version of a product. Construction refers to the set of policies and procedures that, when followed, result in the creation of a specific version of the product. The following two sections address each of these categories in more detail.

5.4.3.2   Version Management

As mentioned earlier, version management refers to the set of policies and procedures that control the creation of a particular version of a product. For example, imagine an application that consists of hundreds, if not thousands, of individual source files. During the development of the next major release of the product, existing source files are changed: Some may be deleted, and new source files may be added. At some point in time, a final build of the product is made based on a policy, or set of rules, that define the specific set of files to be used to produce that specific version of the product.

An example of a version management policy is that maintenance releases will contain only defect repairs made to the product since the last release. Another example: A patch release will contain only the changes made to the product to repair the specific defect that the patch was designed to repair. The procedures followed to enforce such policies vary depending on the CM system being used.

Your customers may not care if a maintenance release contains only defect repairs made to the product since the last release. If they do, that is, it's an element of their quality attributes set, then specifying and enforcing a version management policy is a necessity. CM tools can make it easier to enforce such policies but are certainly not required. If they don't care, you may still want to have and enforce such policies simply to be consistent. In the long run, consistency can help create a perception that your company has its act together.

5.4.3.3 Construction

As mentioned earlier, construction refers to the set of policies and procedures that, when followed, result in the creation of the specific version of the product identified through enforcement of the version management policies discussed in the previous section. An example of a construction policy is that products will be built on systems that are used solely for the purpose of constructing the product. Such a policy is designed to prevent the product from being tainted by unofficial or intermediate versions of libraries, for example. Another example: The product must be built using an optimizing compiler set at maximum optimization and it must be built with full debug information.

Again, if your customers include construction-specific items within their quality attributes set, they can then be addressed through the creation and enforcement of a product construction policy. Otherwise, such a policy may be defined and enforced for consistency. In other words, if full optimization is turned on for one release and then off for the next, the performance regression experienced by your customers may lead to customer dissatisfaction.

5.4.4   Problem/Defect Tracking

Many of the metrics discussed in Chapter 4 can be used only if problems/defects are tracked. For example, *defect arrival rate, defect backlog,* and *backlog management index* are all examples of metrics that can be used only if problems/defects are tracked.

Tracking can be performed using a pad of paper and a pencil, a flat file, a spreadsheet, or a system designed specifically for problem/defect tracking. The first three can be used for smaller projects and smaller teams. However, for larger projects and teams, a more sophisticated system is almost always a necessity.

Among the systems designed specifically for this task, feature sets vary significantly. The simplest of them are best characterized as basic record keeping systems that capture basic information. More sophisticated systems include mechanisms that allow you to assign problems/defects to certain individuals who are then automatically notified by E-mail or pager that an assignment has been made. Usually, such systems support some facility to move the defect through various states, for example, from "new" to "open" to "resolved" to "verified." The most advanced systems are integrated with the source code control and production systems and provide ways to link problem/defect reports with source modules and files.

Regardless of which system you choose, it should be clear that a system is almost always a necessity for practitioners of customer-oriented quality assurance. Without such a system, the metrics at your disposal would be limited to those outside the realm of metrics that rely on information such as the number of unresolved problems/defects outstanding, or the number of problems/defects repaired during some period of time.

5.5   CONCLUSION

The goal of this chapter was to examine various activities that you and your organization can engage in and tools you can use to assist you with the production of a product that satisfies customer quality requirements.

The establishment of and adherence to a development process and the use of configuration management are two necessary components of a successful customer-oriented software quality assurance program. As you will see in the next chapter, they also prepare your organization for evaluation and subsequently, growth.

Chapter 6

Appraisal Programs

6.1 INTRODUCTION

There are few who will argue against the statement that, in general, the quality of software produced in the world today is on the decline. In fact, it has become such a problem that many companies will not purchase "mission-critical" software products from a software vendor unless that vendor measures up against some well-known quality standard or has implemented a formal quality improvement program. Their belief is that such organizations produce products of higher quality. However, measuring up against a well-known quality standard or having a quality improvement program is not sufficient. Remember the premise behind customer-oriented quality assurance: Your customers are the ultimate judge of your product's quality.

Your customers may require you to be registered as an ISO 9000 compliant organization or to have reached a certain rung on the Software Engineering Institute's ladder of capability maturity; however, if you fail to satisfy the remainder of their quality requirements, in their minds, the quality of your product will be inferior. I can cite a number of cases where I have used products that have been produced by an ISO 9000 organization, but whose quality, by my standards, is inferior to that of an unregistered competitor. I can also cite a number of cases where I have used products from an organization that is very mature with respect to the CMM, but whose quality is poor relative to an organization at the very bottom of the CMM.

If you are in the process of obtaining registration to ISO 9000 or if you are developing or following a program designed to mature your product development process, don't stop. But, remember that they are not the final answer to the question: "How can my company improve the quality of its products?" The answer to that question is to put your customers at the center of whatever effort or initiative you are embarking on to improve the quality of your products. Understand what their wants and needs are with respect to quality. Then, build a program that will allow you to deliver products to them that will ultimately satisfy those requirements. If it includes registration to ISO 9000 or something similar, then make that part of your program; otherwise, it's just nice to have.

The remaining sections of this chapter examine two of many quality-oriented appraisal programs: SEI's CMM and the International Organization for Standardization's ISO 9000. The SEI's CMM is designed not only to determine an organization's current level of process maturity, but also to assist that organization in its efforts to improve or mature its process. The primary purpose behind registering to ISO 9000 is to ensure that an organization's quality assurance process includes all of the elements considered necessary by the standard and that its process is documented, followed, and effective. These programs are not mutually exclusive. In other words, you may pursue both an effort to determine your organization's current level of maturity and the development of a plan to move it to a higher level and obtain registration to ISO 9000.

Individually or together, both programs require an organizationwide commitment. If they are not necessary, in other words, if your customers do not explicitly require either, then your investment may be better spent elsewhere. These programs are not bandaids nor are they panaceas. The best QA program is the one that satisfies your customers' quality requirements.

6.2 SOFTWARE ENGINEERING INSTITUTE'S CAPABILITY MATURITY MODEL

6.2.1 History of the SEI's CMM

In 1986, the U.S. federal government funded a project led by the Software Engineering Institute at Carnegie-Mellon University, under the direction of Watts Humphrey and in collaboration with the MITRE Corporation, to develop a software organization appraisal program. The government was looking for a way to determine the capability of software vendors from which it purchased its software. In 1987, the SEI published its appraisal program. Four years later, after extensive research, practical application, and refinement of this original work, the SEI published the Capability Maturity Model. It was revised again in 1993.

6.2.2 Capability Maturity Model

The capability maturity model defines five levels of organizational/process maturity. The levels, listed from least capable to most capable, are

> Level 1 Initial
>
> Level 2 Repeatable
>
> Level 3 Defined
>
> Level 4 Managed
>
> Level 5 Optimizing

At the *initial* level, or Level 1, of maturity, there is a noticeable lack of formality within the organization. Processes may exist but are not followed consistently. Sophisticated tools may be available but are used

---

[1] Mark C. Paulk, et al., *The Capability Maturity Model: Guidelines for Improving the Software Process* (Reading, MA: Addison-Wesley Publishing Company, 1995), p. 5.

[2] Edward Yourdon, *Decline and Fall of the American Programmer* (Englewood Cliffs, NJ: Prentice Hall, 1993), pp. 74–83.

whimsically. Also, project schedules, resource require-ments, and cost are rarely, if ever, accurately predicted.

The members of a Level 1 organization can be thought of as artists. Each follows their own feelings and intuition and draw upon prior experiences when developing a product rather than a common set of pro-cesses and procedures designed specifically for the organization.

A good analogy to use to characterize a Level 1 organization is that it's like playing roulette. You can employ every technique and trick known to mankind to try to make that little ball land in the slot that you pick, but in the end, winning is just a matter of luck.

The *repeatable*, or Level 2, organization is one in which formality prevails. Processes exist and are fol-lowed consistently. Sophisticated tools are available and consistently used across the organization. Project schedules, resource requirements, and cost are almost always accurately predicted. Though processes exist and are consistently followed, they may not be docu-mented or not documented in such a way that an out-sider could come into the organization, refer to the documentation, and with little assistance fit right into and become a productive member of the operation.

The members of a Level 2 organization can be thought of as craftsmen and craftsmen apprentices. A craftsman is someone who practices a skill or trade in some commonly accepted way with little, if any, super-vision. A craftsman apprentice is someone who is learn-ing the skill or trade by closely following and emulating the work of a craftsman. Once an apprentice achieves a certain level of consistency and competency that allows him or her to work independently, they are "promoted" to craftsman. The skill or trade that they practice is not necessarily documented. If you interviewed each member of a team of craftsmen and craftsmen apprentices and asked them to describe the processes and procedures that they follow to produce the product of their craft, they will all give you roughly the same answer. There may be some differences; however, they generally follow the same set of processes and procedures.

The *defined* organization, or Level 3 organization, is distinguished from its predecessor by the existence of formal documentation that details processes and procedures followed by the organization to produce its products. The documentation is also very comprehensive and thorough; in other words, an outsider could come into the organization, refer to the documentation, and with little assistance fit right into and become a productive member of the operation. When the members of the organization are asked to describe the processes and procedures that they follow, they consistently refer to the formal documentation. Beyond serving as a "how-to" guide, the formal documentation establishes a baseline against which efforts to improve the process and procedures can be measured.

The *managed* organization, or Level 4 organization, is one that has defined a set of process metrics for the purpose of someday establishing a continuous improvement program. This is only possible because the product development and qualification processes and procedures are well documented and consistently followed across the organization and from project to project. The focus of the Level 4 organization is on its processes and procedures and the establishment of a formal process metrics program. The focus on lower-level organizations is almost exclusively on the product.

Last, but by no means least, the *optimizing* organization, or Level 5 organization, is one that is primarily focused on process improvement. From project to project, the organization uses its process metrics to fine-tune its processes and procedures. There is no discrete end to continuous improvement. The idea behind continuous improvement is that the processes and procedures followed will continuously evolve into successively higher states of efficiency and effectiveness.

6.2.3 Assessment versus Evaluation

The SEI makes a distinction between assessment and evaluation. Assessment is a less formal process ". . . performed in an open, collaborative environment. . . The objective is to surface problems and help managers and engineers improve their organization." On the other hand, evaluations ". . . are performed in a more audit-oriented environment. The objective is tied to monetary considerations, since the team's recommendation will help select contractors or set award fees."

If you choose to seek an SEI CMM appraisal, the first step is to select the form of appraisal. The decision should be driven by customer quality requirements. If they require organizations that they purchase products from to have a program of self-improvement then the first form of appraisal may be used as a first step in

---

[3] Mark C. Paulk, et al., *The Capability Maturity Model: Guidelines for Improving the Software Process* (Reading, MA: Addison-Wesley Publishing Company, 1995), p. 86.

developing such a program. If, on the other hand, they require a SEI CMM evaluation, then an evaluation from an accredited third-party evaluation agency should be sought.

6.3 INTERNATIONAL ORGANIZATION FOR STANDARDIZATION'S ISO 9000 QUALITY SYSTEM STANDARD

6.3.1 Introduction

The International Organization for Standardization is a consortium of standards bodies representing nearly all the industrialized nations of the world. ISO 9000 is a quality system standard that focuses on process rather than product. The standard does not specify or dictate any particular set of processes or procedures. It does, however, require an organization's quality-oriented functions to engage in a three-part repeating cycle of planning, control, and documentation. The primary objective of the standard is that an organization's quality system provide a high level of confidence that the product produced via that system meets customer expectations and requirements.

6.3.2 History of ISO 9000

As mentioned previously, the ISO 9000 standard is a quality system standard that focuses on process rather

---

[4] Perry L. Johnson, *ISO 9000 Meeting the New International Standards* (New York, NY: McGraw-Hill, Inc., 1993), p. 6.

than product. Its origin can be traced back to the American Department of Defense standard MIL-Q-9858, adopted in 1959 and later revised and called MIL-Q-9858A in 1963. In 1968, NATO adopted MIL-Q-9858A as its own standard for quality systems and called it AQAP-1. Two years later, the British Department of Defense adopted most of AQAP-1, calling it DEF/STAN 05-8. In 1979 Britain officially adopted a standard published by the British Standards Institute called BS 5750, a quality systems standard based on AQAP-1, DEF/STAN 05-8, and MIL-Q-9858A. Finally, in 1987, the International Organization for Standardization published its own standard for quality systems, ISO 9000, based on Britain's BS 5750.

6.3.3 Key Elements of the ISO 9000 Standard

The ISO 9000 standard is, in fact, the parent of three other standards known as ISO 9001, 9002, and 9003. Each of these standards addresses the unique nature of certain classes of organizations. For example, ISO 9001 is specifically designed for use by organizations that design or develop, produce, install, and service products. ISO 9002 is specifically designed for organizations that produce products designed by other companies. Finally, ISO 9003 is specifically designed for organizations that perform inspections of or test products produced by others.

---

[5] Ibid. pp.14–16.

In this book, our primary interest is in ISO 9001. It includes 20 different sections covering various elements of the quality system.[6]

1. Management Responsibility
2. Quality System
3. Contract Review
4. Design Control
5. Document Control
6. Purchasing
7. Purchaser-supplied Product
8. Product Identification and Traceability
9. Process Control
10. Inspection and Testing
11. Inspection, Measuring, and Test Equipment
12. Inspection and Test Status
13. Control of Non-conforming Product
14. Corrective Action
15. Handling, Storage, Package, and Delivery
16. Quality Records
17. Internal Quality Audits
18. Training
19. Servicing [6]
20. Statistical Techniques

As this list suggests, the standard is quite comprehensive. Though it does not specify "how" it is very spe-

---

[6] Ibid., pp.37-39.

cific about "what." For example, Section 1 *Management Responsibility* specifies the following requirements checklist:

- Management designates a representative with authority and responsibility for implementing and maintaining the requirements of the standard.

- Management establishes documents and publicizes its policy, objectives, and commitment to quality and customer satisfaction.

- Management defines the responsibility, authority, and relationships for all employees whose work affects quality.

- Management conducts in-house verification and review of the quality systems.

It should be obvious from the requirements checklist above that for this standard to be successfully implemented and maintained, a substantial time and human resource commitment must be made at the very highest levels of management, if not the highest level. Before pursuing ISO 9000 registration, it may be prudent to invest in an informal assessment to estimate the short-term and long-term costs. Then, weigh those findings against the potential loss of revenue due to lack of ISO 9000 registration. If the return on investment justifies the costs, then you have a strong business case for pursuing registration.

---

[7] Ibid., p. 46.

6.3.4 To Register or Not to Register

Like the SEI's CMM, there are two kinds of appraisal associated with ISO 9000. One form of appraisal, and the less formal of the two, is performed for reasons other than to seek formal quality process registration. For example, an organization may simply desire to assess its readiness for registration or simply as part of a process improvement program. Such an appraisal is performed by an agency other than an official registration agency, known as a Notified Body. It may be performed by an inside agency or an outside agency knowledgeable about the process of registration.

The other form of appraisal is known as registration. It is always performed by an official outside registration agent known as a *registrar*. The registrar audits an organization's process and documentation to determine if the organization satisfies or complies with the standard. If registration is granted, registration is maintained through semiannual visits from the registrar. At these visits, the registrar determines whether or not registration should be maintained or revoked.

There are a number of reasons why you may or may not want to register. If the organization, more importantly the market at large, requires registration, then your choice is limited to register and remain competitive or not to register and watch your revenues drop into the abyss. If, however, your customers and prospects have no short-term or long-term requirement for ISO 9000 registration, then registration is optional.

Assessment, in this case, becomes a diagnostic tool for organizational self-improvement.

6.4 CONCLUSION

If you were not already familiar with these appraisal programs prior to reading this chapter, hopefully, you have a better appreciation for the amount of effort behind them. Whether or not you choose to pursue either, or some other program, the questions that you should ask before forging down this path are: "Am I doing this to satisfy customer quality requirements?" and "If not, where else might my investment be made that will allow me to achieve greater results with respect to satisfying their quality requirements?"

---

[8] Ibid., pp. 24–25.

Conclusion

This book addressed and provided a means by which an organization can solve several common problems faced when producing software products:

- Complex software systems having hundreds of millions of possible test cases and test scenarios are rarely, if ever, completely tested due to the practical constraints of time and resources. How does one select a sufficient subset of tests and test scenarios so that the quality of the end product satisfies the customer?

- Metrics are used throughout the software industry to gauge product quality. A metric is a measurement with an associated desirable value. For example, the defects per thousand lines of code measurement has an associated desirable value of less than one defect per million lines of code. If a product has one defect per ten thousand lines of code, is its quality poor? Also, does this measurement ultimately mean anything? Or, is it more important to measure the impact those defects have on the customer as they use the product? How does one select the right metrics to gauge product quality?

- Tests are the primary means by which product quality is assessed. What does it mean when a test fails? Is the quality of the product poor? Perhaps, but ultimately the value of a test lies in its ability to determine whether or not the product satisfies customer quality requirements. For example, is a test that places a load on the system five times greater than any customer will ever place on the system a good determinant of quality? How does one select the right tests to use?

- There are a number of popular quality assurance appraisal programs advocated today. Charged with selecting one, which is the best to follow?

I hope I have convinced you that to answer the questions above, you must listen to your customers. Understand their wants and needs with respect to quality. Satisfy them and you will achieve the greatest level of quality possible. Also, I hope that I have convinced you that there is no single formula for success when it comes to quality. Again, your best chance for success is to put your customers at the center of any effort that you embark on designed to improve the quality of your products.

Finally, I would love to hear from anyone who attempts to apply what they have learned in this book to a real-world scenario. Please contact the publisher for information on how to contact me through E-mail.

Bibliography

Carnegie-Mellon University/Software Engineering Institute. *The Capability Maturity Model: Guidelines for Improving the Software Process*. Reading, MA: Addison-Wesley Publishing Company, 1995.

Jenner, Michael. *Software Quality Management and ISO 9001: How to Make Them Work For You*. New York: John Wiley and Sons, 1995.

Johnson, Perry. *ISO 9000: Meeting the New International Standards*. New York: McGraw-Hill, 1993.

Kan, Stephen. *Metrics and Models in Software Quality Engineering.* Reading, MA: Addison-Wesley Publishing Company, 1995.

Kidder, Tracy. *The Soul of a New Machine.* New York: Avon Books, 1981.

Kotler, Philip, and Gary Armstrong. *Principles of Marketing,* 5th ed. Englewood Cliffs, NJ: Prentice Hall, 1991.

Lorenz, Mark, and Jeff Kidd. *Object-Oriented Software Metrics.* Englewood Cliffs, NJ: Prentice Hall, 1994.

Moore, David, and George McCabe. *Introduction to the Practices of Statistics,* 2nd ed. New York: W.H. Freeman and Company, 1993.

Yourdon, Edward. *The Decline and Fall of the American Programmer.* Englewood Cliffs, NJ: Prentice Hall, 1993.

Index